HARR\

QUEST FOR SILENCE

Quest for Silence

Harry A. Wilmer

DAIMON

We thank the Mary Weir Trust Fund for partially subsidizing this book.

Cover illustration: At the top of the picture is the All-seeing eye of Horus, the Egyptian Sky god. Below the eye there are two large intersecting circles with a mandola in the center of the picture. At the top of the mandola is a white equilateral triangle. Euclid's Proposition #1, from *Elements* shows this diagram as a critical figure in his geometry. The lower part of the mandola becomes a shield of red upon which is placed a silver Welch Dragon which I bought in Wales just before I began this yarn picture. In the upper left hand corner is a silver American eagle which I place in each of my pictures as a symbol of soaring imagination and insight. Under the circles is a large Black Hole of the death of a star, a tunnel or a vagina. The top light blue sky is countered below by deep dark blue and brilliant red and violet with a white fringe suggesting the Swiss Alps. The tidy grey bow at the bottom of the shield represents the aesthetic principle. The two connecting white triangles at the lower edges of the yellow eyes are like a face and helmet each with a bloody decoration at the peak suggesting violence and aggression. I made this yarn picture in October 1999.

To the late Mary Weir, M.D., Ph.D., friend, student and analysand, devoted to the public understanding of the psychology of C. G. Jung. Mary was a gifted psychiatrist and remarkable human being.

There is no use whatsoever writing a book unless you know that you must write that book or go mad, or perhaps die.
— Robertson Davies
The Merry Heart

Harry Wilmer and Mitten

CONTENTS

Preface

In his collection of essays on literary criticism, *Language and Silence*, written in the nineteen-sixties, George Steiner writes:

> What I have been aiming at, throughout, is the notion of humane literacy ... where it is more than reverie or an indifferent appetite sprung of boredom, reading is a mode of action (p. 10). Because the community of traditional values is splintered, because words themselves have been twisted and cheapened ... the art of reading, of true literacy, must be reconstituted. It is the task of literary criticism to help us read as total human beings ... (p. 11).

More often than not, moving into modern technocracy, it is through psychological doctors like Harry Wilmer that we have found the way to this new humanism, where action generated from the unconscious provides the humane literacy George Steiner envisages. Although Dr. Wilmer is a skilled writer, his writings are informed by significant actions in the world, well summarized by Elizabeth Silverthorne in her Foreword.

Outstanding is his achievement of establishing the type of treatment known as a therapeutic community for mental illness, which he did in the Navy in Oakland (CA) and at the Langely Porter Clinic in San Francisco. On a totally different level of expertise, he founded the Institute for the Humanities at Salado, Texas. Here, he gave of himself to others so that speakers of all kinds could add their contribution to his own model of humane literacy. As a onetime participant at Salado,

I also experienced the fullness of his gift for attracting local people to hear his speakers in an atmosphere of acceptance that was social in the best sense, and, of course, it honored that meaningful silence that is the creative source of true communication.

Joseph L. Henderson
Ross, California

A Letter from the Publisher

Valentine's Day, 1993

Dear Harry,

...

Regarding my own thoughts on silence (not unrelated to certain aspects of Wilderness): because my thesis work ended up going in a different direction, I never took the 'silence' idea very far, at least in writing – I wish I had, and I may still someday try. I have no doubt that it is the very paucity of silences in my own life that has kept me from adequately pursuing this subject, and indeed my writing in general. Ironically, it would seem, it is in silence, in the absence of stimulus, that space exists for a kind of communion; but a different communion than that of non-silence. In silence, we can be in touch with whatever it is that we need to be in touch with, within or without, and which, in the absence of silence, would be lost. My own greatest source of 'silence' is the alpine forest walk, to which I occasionally treat myself, though not often enough, as I realize again and again. It is not 'silent' at all in the strict sense of the word, but it provides the kind of silence my soul needs for regeneration.

I have noticed again and again that it is often a silence somewhere in the course of an analysis which brings a breakthrough, a transformation, a new level of trust. I have never forgotten how, in an early session with one of my very first analysands many years ago, I sensed that to speak would be a kind of violation: and so I remained silent for the entire hour, as did she, something I had never done before, and never have done since. After she departed, I began to doubt my having been silent, telling myself I probably should have 'helped' her to express herself by asking her questions, or just saying something to 'break the ice,' as it were. I concluded there was a very good chance I would never see her again. However: she appeared a few days later for her next session, positively *beaming* and happily told me how vitally important that hour of silence had been for her. She said it was the first time in her life that she felt nothing whatsoever was being demanded of her: she could just be – silent and accepted as she was. This experience marked a major turning-point in her life. And it confirmed for me the healing function that silence can have.

Of course, the discussion could go on and on, bringing in *negative* aspects of silence as well, its place in time, different forms of silence, etc. – but I imagine you're probably well into the subject by now, and way ahead of me, so I'll stop here, in anticipation of hearing your ideas in December, and reading them whenever your book comes out. I'm greatly looking forward to both!

At about the same time as your letter, TIME magazine arrived here with a 1-page essay by Pico Iyer entitled, "The Eloquent Sounds of Silence," which contains some beautiful quotations and ideas – I suppose you probably already have it, but in case you don't, I enclose a photocopy for you. And of course you know "The Sounds of Silence" by Simon and Garfunkel, which, in its extolling of some of the beauties of silence probably has helped many to become a little more aware.

All best wishes in your 'silent endeavors,'
and warm regards,
Bob

P.S. It was Liliane Frey here in Zürich who originally suggested the 'silence' topic to me some 17 or 18 years ago, saying that it is such an important phenomenon, yet it receives so little attention. To the best of my knowledge, however, she didn't put her ideas to paper, unfortunately.

Man can almost be defined as a species with only exceedingly limited and falsifying access to the universe (for it is nothing less) of silence.

– George Steiner
No Passion Spent

Foreword

To speak of silence at book length may seem at first a paradox, but Harry Wilmer soon reveals it as a subject of fascinating ramifications. Consciously and unconsciously, he has been researching the themes of silence and listening for most of his life.

At the age of seven, having discarded the dreams of being a fireman or policeman, Harry decided to be a physician. From this dream he never wavered. Born in New Orleans, Louisiana, on March 5, 1917, he grew up in a family in which his father, a successful businessman, ruled in an aristocratic and autocratic paterfamilias manner. This approach was an ordeal to his independent-minded son. Despite their heated arguments, in which the elder Wilmer always had the last word, he was an affectionate father who enjoyed taking his son on camping trips. He was extremely proud of his son's bright mind and the honors and awards he began to collect at an early age. As he foresaw, his son was destined to become a brilliant doctor.

In contrast to his father's control through words, Harry's mother's method of control and authority was through silence. Her silent treatment was often sufficient to exact obedience (if not acquiescence) from young Harry, who could not bear to feel he didn't exist in her eyes. She, too, greatly admired doctors and encouraged his ambition to enter the medical profession.

When Harry was five, the family moved to Minneapolis, Minnesota, where his father became manager of Fulton Bag and Cotton Mills. In the center of the business floor, his father's large, glassed-in office seemed like an oasis. On the factory's upper floors, row after row of monstrous machines spun fabric to make cotton bags for flour mills. Young Harry was proud to be the boss's son, but the deafening roar of the machines was unnerving to the child. It seemed a ferocious repetitious cycle of senseless racket. One afternoon when Harry heard the machines turn off, the silence that followed was overwhelming.

Among Harry senior's acquaintances in Minnesota were the Mayo brothers, and he arranged for his thirteen-year-old son to meet them. To the young boy, they were like gods who dwelt on the Olympian heights of the shrine that was the Mayo Clinic. His feelings never changed – not through the training he took there, nor through serving on the staff, nor through all the years of holding important positions in various prestigious institutions. Mayo is where he has always returned in time of serious illness and the place "strongest" in his heart.

The extraordinary energy and ability that characterize Harry Wilmer are reflected in his rapid transit through educational channels. He earned a bachelor's degree in two years, both a medical and a master's degree in four years, and a Ph.D. in two years. During this same time, he published eight scientific papers and two books.

When Harry became disillusioned with Freudian training (just at the point of completing it), he gave away his couch and became a Jungian. His thinking, however, has not been limited to following any one leader blindly. He has listened carefully to the great leaders of many philosophies and selected from each the best guides for his psyche. One example is his adoption of the Tao – the way, the middle path, both spiritually and earthly in which the inner world is one with the outer.

Life-threatening illnesses have deepened Harry's understanding of silence. When he fell victim to tuberculosis in

1941, it was known as the "White Plague" and the killer of many young doctors. A heavy stigma and shroud of silence increased the emotional and spiritual isolation of the patients who were treated by strict bed rest and in total isolation at that time. There were no drugs.

Harry's response was to lift the shroud of silence by writing a book, *Huber the Tuber: The Lives and Loves of a Tubercle Bacillus*, with humorous text and cartoons explaining the nature of the disease.

Undergoing heart surgery and realizing that his own heart had been removed from his body for several hours led to renewed contemplation about the significance of being capable of listening to the sounds of our bodies. The surreal silence following the deep anesthetic void, the enforced silence of not being able to speak because of an endotracheal tube, and the helpless feeling of being strapped down – speechless and in pain – made him aware that he had come as close to the ultimate silent state as one can be in life.

Following this experience he built his greenhouse, a retreat where he can find solitude and quiet in the company of Mitten, his silent totem cat, yet still be within a few minutes of Jane, his beloved wife for over fifty years. In this retreat, as in his home study and in his office at the Institute for the Humanities at Salado, are mementos reflecting numerous journeys to far-off places and hundreds of hours spent in the company of great minds, past and present. Here, too, are gifts reflecting the gratitude of patients and friends whose lives he has touched.

For a number of years, Harry suffered an intermittent depression, even as he continued to receive recognition and honors in his field. With the understanding help of his Jungian analyst, Joseph Henderson, he eventually overcame the depression. Even though the state helped him better understand how to help his own patients, the perceived necessity of keeping silent about it – as a psychiatrist – was an added burden.

The reverse of silence is the need to speak out when silence is creating evil. In the 1940s and 1950s, Harry was distressed by the cruel treatment, including the use of harsh restraints and isolation, of patients with severe mental illnesses. At that time, he was in the navy, so he obtained permission to establish a therapeutic community at the U.S. Naval Hospital in Oakland, California. Here patients could speak out and be listened to. His work was recognized by naval officers, including Admiral Chester Nimitz who, after observing his navy ward, said, "A valuable new technique has been added to the resources for treating severe mental illness ... representing new horizons of hope. ..."

Harry wrote several articles and a book, *Social Psychiatry in Action*, based on his experiences with this new therapy. From his book, a television docudrama was created: *People Need People*, narrated by Fred Astaire, starring Lee Marvin, and featuring Arthur Kennedy as Wilmer. It was nominated for five Emmy awards, and shown nationally and on BBC London. Material for the book was also used in a three-act play.

Harry also had major surgery at the Mayo Clinic for cancer of the prostate with hope and cure, another intimate experience as a patient. His work with Vietnam veterans is another instance of breaking an evil silence. By dealing with their nightmares and encouraging them to break the silence that a feeling of rejection had created, Harry opened up a potential for healing. During his professorship at the University of Texas Health Sciences Center at San Antonio, he created a therapeutic community for schizophrenic patients and began his work on a book to be called *The Healing Nightmare*.

For several years, Harry asked patients to tell him their feelings about silence. Throughout this volume are vignettes of what they revealed about their experiences with and their dreams about silence. In everyday language, they discuss the spiritual good potential of silence and its shadowy bad potential. Another motif consists of quotations in poetry and prose from great writers of the East and the West who have recorded their observations on the subject. From his vast reading and deep meditation, Harry has included the wisdom of ancient and modern philosophers on the blessings of silence and solitude.

He opens up for us the possibility of learning by listening *into* silence, and makes us aware of the importance of the silent spaces between our words and the silent spaces in our relationships. He reminds us of the silence of death and the silence necessary to hear the voice of God.

Finally, Harry shows us the potential of solitude as a sanctuary to shut out the noisy world in order to become creative and whole again. He says that the dangerous American compulsion to be gap fillers has come about because we are afraid of silence – the most important factor in conversation, art, and music.

As we begin to agree with Cowper, "How sweet, how passing sweet, is solitude," we may wish that we, too, had a familiar being like Mitten to share our moments of solitary bliss.

Elizabeth Silverthorne

*Everyone among them talks; no one knows
how to understand any more. Everyone falls
into the water, nothing falls into deep wells
any longer.*
*Everyone among them talks; nothing turns
out well any more and is finished. Everyone
cackles; but who wants to sit quietly in the
nest and hatch eggs?*
*Everyone among them talks; everything is
talked to pieces. And what even yesterday
was still hard for time itself and its tooth,
hangs, spoiled by scraping and gnawing, out
of the mouths of men today.*
*Everyone among them talks; everything is
betrayed, and what was once called secret
and the secrecy of deep souls today belongs to
the street trumpeters and other butterflies.
Oh, everything human is strange, a noise on
dark streets! But now it lies behind me again:
my greatest danger lies behind me.*

– Friedrich Wilhelm Nietzsche
Thus Spake Zarathustra

1

A Gap-Filling Society

America is a nation of gap fillers and space pluggers. We are individuals who usually do not listen to other people. We talk all the time, even when others are talking. People are deluged by radio and television. We awaken and we go to sleep caught up in gossip, news of violence, and people acting funny interrupted by high-pitched bursts of loud laughter.

Our social lives are a mélange of noise. We settle for lighthearted, flickering relationships and recreational sins, and revel in offensive talk on the electronic media carnival. The computer has invaded our central nervous systems.

We talk over each other. Americans want to be on top and give as little space as possible to others. We are conditioned by the consequences of the high costs of time-space on television, where fast talkers get more in for the money while audiences listen marginally. The commercials are high state-of-the-art American gap fillers.

In the 1930s, I had a sound-effect record for use on radio. It was filled with assorted bursts of laughter, canned laughter, to be played after a joke or an event that was supposed to be funny. Joke, technician flips on instant guffaws, and bursts of laughter prove the jokesters are funny. Today, live studio audiences are warmed up before the show is on the air, and cued to laugh on signals. It is laughter on demand.

When I listen to programs like *Good Morning America*, the riles of laughter from the performers and the audience are quick and loud. It sounds to me exactly like old records of cackling canned laughter. Such a production simulates extra-verted euphoria. Maybe this type of TV and radio subtly reminds us that we are laughing at ourselves.

Without pauses or silent spaces for humor to sink in, Americans disown the slow-take as an English sense of humor. To add to the tension, people are talking fast, talking over, and interrupting each other in hilarious, noisy free-for-alls.

The same cacophony of noise characterizes restaurants that are poorly soundproofed. For people like me, with hearing aids, the noise is physically painful and the words mostly indecipherable. I suspect this ambience is a deliberate business ploy so that seated customers talk less, and waiting customers can take the vacated table. The space you occupy is a gap to be refilled as soon and as often as possible. At the other extreme, there are slow-paced, posh restaurants where meals seem to go on interminably and intimate conversation is apt to be self-conscious and stuffy-slow.

Silent spaces spoil cocktail parties. No one goes to a cocktail party for a thoughtful conversation. Rather than human connectedness, talk-talk-hook-ups characterize the communication. We are a nation in love with noise, equating it with progress, action, power, and influence. It must fill every crack because we are afraid of silence.

City air is full of fumes, smoke, smog, and radioactive and toxic waste. Desiring the Garden of Eden, we have a nostalgia for crystal-pure running water and the invigorating crisp morning air in the wilderness.

People love what is rare and scarce like precious silences associated with naturally paced life. We look with awe and wonderment into the black night sky with the countless sparkling white points of stars. The dark sky stretching on forever gives us a sense of ultimate silence, of creation and of death.

What happened to silence? Nothing happened to silence. It is always there, has always been there, and always will be there. At any time and everywhere, it is ready to become known the moment we stop filling the gaps that hide it. A commercial is called a plug. When a person's mouth is open, saying nothing, a gap is exhibited.

It is said that Nature abhors a vacuum, instantly filling it up as soon as it is found. A vacuum is a confined space theoretically devoid of matter, or a space from which gas has been evacuated. Thus, a vacuum is defined by what it is not – the absent contents. We think that silence is the absence of sound and we call annoying talk "vacuous."

This discussion leads me to the so-called Silent Treatment, a nonverbal aggressive way of shutting up another person until he or she capitulates. It is a power game that is manifested in its purest form by two human beings not talking to each other. The more powerful authoritarian person will not speak until the other capitulates. This treatment is conditional love.

It is as if I say that I will withhold my love and feelings until you give into what I expect or demand. I love you, not as you are, but only if you are not whom you really are. Silent treatment of children by mothers is more dramatic than with fathers, where it is often demonstrated by withdrawal, isolation, or threatening dissociation. The core issue for the child is: Do I exist?

William James wrote:

> No more fiendish torture could be devised than when you speak, no one answers; when you wave, no one turns; but everybody simply cuts you dead. Soon there wells up within you such hostility you attack those who ignore you, and, if that fails to bring you recognition, you turn your hostility on yourself in an effort to prove you really do exist.[1]

I speak with personal authority on this subject, remembering the anguish I felt when my mother gave me the silent treatment and my father criticized me whenever I tried to

---

[1]Carpenter, Edmund. *They Became What They Beheld*. New York: Ballantine Books, 1970.

stand up for my own ideas with him. My mother could maintain an adamantine stony silence for hours or days until I could no longer stand the tension and the feeling that I did not exist in her world. Then, having appeased her, I gave up. Silent treatment is filling a huge gap with a palpable silence in a mean-spirited attitude for the child's own good.

It took me decades to learn to speak for myself and not be intimidated by authoritarian voices or to seek benevolent authorities or truly great people. When one person refuses to speak to another until that person capitulates by renouncing his or her own truth, this is coercion. To accept sham as if it were truth, to confess that what you do not believe is the truth, is a form of brainwashing under which we learn hypocrisy and sham to survive in our sham-full world.

A child usually carries on this parental legacy when the parents are no longer there. It is internalized. We do it to ourselves. The adults or children are at the mercy of others who were rewarded for filling all the gaps with words – challenging, arguing, shouting – the outgoing extrovert bullies.

Since I was a small child, I had two talents to compensate for the imposed silence: I could write or I could paint and draw. Today I am most content when I am writing or painting – alone. During my professional career, I have published thirteen books and over two hundred scientific articles, mostly as the sole author – a very unusual aspect in today's medical and scientific world. I am obviously speaking for myself. In my helping role as a psychiatrist or analyst, I am intrigued by patients who have suffered this same kind of abuse.

A Case in Point

A middle-aged woman whom I shall call Jeannette consulted me because of despair and a painful feeling that she could never accomplish anything of significance. Her life felt hollow and meaningless. It just droned on and on. She was smart, sophisticated, quick of perception, and depressed.

During Jeanette's first meeting, she told me of the accidental death of her unattended infant son in their own swimming pool. For years, she had suffered an unrelenting self-blame and guilt. The tragic story and her nearly irreconcilable feelings of grief and guilt were almost too painful for me to hear. At the beginning of her work with me, she asked if she could audiotape each of our sessions. I agreed.

From the start, I recognized that her speech poured out in endless sentences tied together so tightly that there was no space for me to join in. When I forced myself to interrupt her rapid-fire talk, she would stop – out of a lifelong habit of good manners – to give me space. She received whatever I said with nonchalant indifference, however. This reception distressed me because, frankly, I thought I had some things that were important, maybe even brilliant.

Then the flood of words gushed on from where I had interrupted her. Jeannette's almost impenetrable word defense was like a moat over which she had pulled up the drawbridge in the wall of her castle. Her talking kept me out as if I were a dangerous enemy and not, as I saw it, a helper trying to befriend her.

A different explanation occurred to me that gave me a sense of freedom from being inundated with words – that Jeannette was giving me the silent treatment, but unlike my mother's silent treatment gave me not the slightest hint about how I could capitulate. This situation meant that I had a countertransference problem in reaction to this woman. I saw myself in the heroic role of her lifesaver, like the heroic role of saving someone who was drowning. The rescue role is a treacherous one for a psychotherapist whose overriding philosophy is to get the patient to save herself while the doctor stands by.

I concluded that her attitude of keeping me from talking about the trauma was right and that my following the traditional analytic pattern of interpretations was wrong. It struck me that Jeannette's speech pattern had an unconscious wisdom. Therefore, I ceased to make any interpretation about her speech as resistance and resolved not to speak of the terrible trauma or even to say the child's name, which seemed taboo. I consciously withheld any explicit explanation or interpretation when I thought from her stream of consciousness the event was the real reference. After a month, Jeannette would talk spontaneously about the death of her son and on rare occasions mention his name.

I listened silently – even more carefully – not to the words but to the speech pattern and rhythm, and tried to guess at its metaphorical meaning. To my disappointment, this different silent listening resulted in Jeannette becoming more depressed. Only in retrospect do I see that this more interactive silent listening was an unconscious form of unwelcome engagement, awakening her fears and depression. I prescribed antidepressant medication that helped, but Jeannette began questioning whether she should end her treatment.

I thought, perhaps, that this highly extraverted woman, by slipping to this low point of depression, was being turned inward in an unpleasant introverted way, forcing her to deep introspection. In other words, this aspect of her depression could be seen as serving a potentially useful purpose. It is a common belief that in certain disorders we must reach a low before we can turn upwards, like the alcoholic who hits rock bottom before taking the responsibility for active steps to recovery, as with Alcoholics Anonymous.

Instead of my responding to Jeannette's fear that her therapy had failed and had no future, I saw this development as my opportunity. I asked her to listen carefully to an idea that had been in my mind for some time.

I explained that her speech sounded as if she were beginning each new sentence before she had finished the last sentence, leaving no between space for me to talk to her. There were no periods. Plenty of ands, buts, thens, ors, you knows, colons, semicolons, commas, and dashes – but no periods or pauses. It was a breathless talk that would be intriguing to her friends. Her separate thoughts may end, but were immediately coupled onto other thoughts. This was a long-time verbal habit of control to avoid the fear of losing control.

Rather than respond to Jeannette's thoughts of ending her analytic work, I asked if she would leave the audiotape of her present therapy hour with me so I could listen to it. Previously she had kept the tapes and listened to them in her car while driving to her visits with me.

I listened to the tape and transcribed it myself, highlighting all the conjunctions with a yellow marking pen. Midway into the next hour, she asked about the tape. I replayed a randomly selected five-minute part and handed her my typed highlighted transcription. Long ago I had realized that five minutes of audiotape dialogue contain about the maximum time that can be comprehended in a session with a patient or a student whom I was supervising. To have played more would have been like my inundating her with words she could not interrupt because I would have my hand on the tape controls. Father again. Jeannette listened intently, looked at my transcript, understood, and was impressed.

Here is part of the transcript:

What you may be able to slither through sometimes *and* get to the Holy *and* there is always the intimidation [sic] of it *but* that is all you get is intimidation *and* so it tends to make you want to be very quiet *and* to make you want to hold your breath *but* you see that won't work either – it's the moment when you shift over *and* the breath goes over the way *and* with the music you get the feeling that when it's very slow music – there's a jazz recording of the Happy Jazz Band *and* they're doing the Ave Maria *but* it is used so much in jazz music *but* it's not that – it's something about the way the artist plays the clarinet that has the intimation of jazz *and yet* the jazz is all white in this sense, a sort of jazz *but* he'll hold his notes for a long time in this *and* then for just a few seconds he will let go because he eases into the next one *and* right up to the break there is the same thing I am talking about *and* it is the same thing that is seeing the long row of columns in a monastery or in a cloister somewhere – your eyes see that *and* break between them *and* there is something in the break that brings in the silence *and* the silence has something to do with the Holy. (Yes, *period*!) That is all I mean. (Period)

Jeannette realized what I was telling her while hearing this tape as she read my transcription of it. The following excerpt from her next session shows how she changed her manner of speaking:

JEANNETTE: "I don't remember my father ever talking to me about anything except giving orders." [Pause] "He never responded to anything I said."

HARRY: "How does it seem talking to me now, in light of what you just said?"

JEANNETTE: "It's very peculiar to me. It makes it so hard to verbalize, like as long as I have someone listening to me, then I must be very careful not to babble. I am sure I believe it. By that I mean I am not sure that you are really listening."

HARRY: "Really? What is babbling?"

JEANNETTE: "Babbling – just responding to life."

HARRY: "Where does the word babble come from?"

JEANNETTE: "The waterfalls. The babbling of the creek."

HARRY: "So. You are supposed to do that. To just talk would be like a babble. A positive babble then?"

JEANNETTE: "Yes. That's very nice. That's a thought I would like to hug. It certainly was never allowed. Since no one listened to me before, I never had to think what I really thought. The stuff could all stay inside. I knew more or less that I thought about things, but that's different from verbalizing."

HARRY: "Then it would be nice to babble."

JEANNETTE: "I think that I have lost that ability."

HARRY: "Have you? Isn't that what you've been doing?"

JEANNETTE: "I am trying. My father never stopped talking, come to think about it. He just didn't want any interference. He wanted to do it all."
HARRY: "And sometimes you?"

I once thought to myself that the silent treatment by a parent – which was in essence what her father did – drowns the child's spirit and makes the child feel that he or she does not exist. I associated it with the silence of the dead child who drowned having to find his voice in his mother. This way of dealing with her grief and sense of guilt was like teaching her how to talk to save herself.

In a fast-paced society, it would be healthy to take time to talk more slowly when you really want other people to listen to you. Be forewarned: Pick your time carefully. You might get your thoughts over with words. Have patience. Remember that talking slowly gives rhythm and space, even melody to speech. Speech needs space to breathe. It is the empty spaces that mark the greatest speakers. Listen to Mark Twain's wisdom: "I'll tell you how to make an ordinary speech, a good speech: 'Learn to make pauses.'"[1]

Silent Gaps

Mark Twain returned a manuscript to his editor who had complained, "There's not enough punctuation marks in the MS." So Mark filled an entire page with semicolons, periods, apostrophes, commas and colons and sent it back to the editor saying, "Here, you put them in."[2]

In a nation of gap fillers, to inflict an open gap on someone is cruel and unusual treatment. It borders on inhuman treatment. The "silent treatment" is a way of imposing silence as a

[1]Twain, Mark. *On Writing and Publishing*. New York: Book of the Month Club, 1994, p. 27ff.
[2]Barzun, Jacques. Seminar at the Institute for the Humanities at Salado (Salado, Texas), November 20, 1988.

palpable object into the field of a relationship. This kind of silence is not the silence that is the essential story of my book. It is a bastardized silence. It is a well-known fact that cruel interrogators, arrogant authorities, and inflated people manifest indifferent coldness to those individuals or groups they perceive as insignificant and unimportant.

The snub is an example of the brief condescending silence that feels as if someone has turned his or her back on you. I have never forgotten an event when I was a young doctor and heard a world-famous physician give a spellbinding oration. At the conclusion of his talk, I joined the people who came forward and crowded around him. When at last it was my turn to speak to him, I told him how deeply his talk had affected me. He looked at me for an instant when I started to talk, then turned his face to his right and looked at other people all the time I was speaking. When I finished, he turned to the next person in line without a word to me. It was as if he had banged his gavel and held me in contempt. At that moment, I vowed I would never again be thrilled enough to march forward to compliment a speaker dwelling in the afterglow of his or her own words.

Tell Me About Silence

I explained to each of my patients that I was writing a book about silence and wished to record our discussion on a tape recorder. I also said that I needed their permission to print parts of the transcripts. Each readily agreed. I personally made all the transcriptions.

A middle-aged successful working woman whom I will call Martha immediately described her mother's cruel use of the silent treatment as discipline. Her father was a passive man who paid little attention to her. She said that he was somewhat in limbo. Even when she reached out, he ignored her and never intervened in the conflicts between Martha's mother and their daughter. Martha was an only child, born with multiple physical disabilities. She obviously felt unwanted.

Martha accepted her mother's silent treatment by total acquiescence, telling me she felt like a slave who could not please her master. Her mother failed to nourish her child, relating to her as a damaged object without feeling. Martha was explicit: "The silent treatment made me feel as if I didn't exist." This feeling affirmed her awareness that she was an unwanted, nonexistent, damaged child. Martha characterized her childhood as desperate. As she grew older, however, instead of giving up and living a life in limbo like her father, she became a determined, courageous woman struggling to prove her existence and individual worth.

Explaining this outcome in terms of mastering silence, she said:

> I think that at a certain point in living it's a necessary task to be silent. If it wasn't for silence, I would have more misery. I think that coming to terms with silence and learning to be silent is a part of having a more complete understanding. The absence of sound is a rarity because if you confine yourself there is always something going on, but if you reach total silence, that, I think, is an ideal state. The silent treatment by my mother was a painful experience coming from an authority figure. I felt some anger and wanted to say, "I'm here, too! I want my turn." It was as if I didn't exist.

Martha added:

> More and more she cut me out of her reactions by my reaction. What helped me was that I survived the war with myself and my mother by building my own space to keep my mother from taking me over. [I would] say to myself, "This is my space. This is mine. I'm going to do it. I am determined." Determination was a way to build my own space. It was like warfare as far as I was concerned. I knew

it took all the energy out of me, battling with myself and my mother. I survived by carving out a separate space.

It is fitting that she sought the beneficent silence in silent contemplation with the Catholic Sisters of Divine Providence. The silence of the convent hinted at the ideal total state. After two years of spiritual direction in addition to our analytic work, Martha could, for the first time, admit explicit malice toward her mother – not merely, "I felt some anger!" She said that when she was a child, her mother would take to bed and do nothing to care for herself. The traditional mother-daughter roles were reversed and she was required to nurture and care for her psychologically invalid mother. She found a new successful career helping people.

Noise Treatment

I asked one of my male patients, a physician, about the silent treatment. He replied, "I didn't get the silent treatment – just the opposite: a torrential word treatment so that I was rendered speechless. My father talked compulsively with endless circumstantiality. He would lecture me nonstop and I would cease to exist. It was as if I had become invisible and spaced out.

> I would focus on my father's tie while Father just relieved himself [sic] on me. I was totally silent. Questioning him or talking back or hitting back was out of the question. I was afraid of him. I said to myself, "This man is dangerous." I was afraid of his temper, his violence. I was unnecessary, just a receptacle. I was silent. I was so inhibited that it was as if I didn't exist.

This doctor had come to me because he wanted to talk to an older man who would patiently listen to him. It would be an antidote against the lecturing father he still carried inside himself. He paid for his treatment out of his pocket, quite correctly not trusting the confidentiality of his health insurance company. It was not too high a price to pay for my silence. The managed care people are obsessive gap fillers, requiring physicians to hand over confidential records which are then available to the police, the federal government, and employers. I never sign an agreement with a managed care insurance company, and silence them.

When Silence Needs a Noisy Companion

One of my patients, whom I will call Jeff, was a senior in college, majoring in anthropology. His response to my question about silence surprised me:

"I can tolerate silence only with noise," he said. "Silence has all the lurking dangers of the darkest forces."

I said nothing, and he finally continued:

> Silence is listening to you talk. I can experience silence, but it is almost as if I had to be distracted to do that. One way I have been able to do that, so that I can understand all that you are talking about, is through drumming, having something in a sense distracting my own thought process.

I was now learning that in his mind while we were talking there were drums beating in his head to trick his noisy mind. To create silence within his mind, he became the trickster beating drums to scare away the demons of noise.

Jeff said:

> Silence to me seems timeless. One is not aware of ticking inside oneself. When I think of silent places, I think first of darkness, peace, and tranquillity. I think of the mountains and I think of the north, like a snowstorm. It seems you have to be blinded or deafened in a way. But noise is

painful and terrifying to me. Even as a child I had a strange dream – I don't know if "dream" is the right word, but it was something that kept recurring periodically throughout my childhood and even in my youth. Even a tiny bit in adulthood. In the dream, there would be physical grinding of my teeth, hearing a sewing machine and a mill grinding. All I can remember is the sound. It was just a sound dream.

Dreams are usually silent. What could be the significance of this recurrent dream of three specific kinds of repetitive mechanical noises with no images?

One does not see anything in the blackest of nights. Because Jeff was an anthropology student, I recalled an observation of Claude Lévi-Strauss about noise:

> As for the din that is made at the time of an eclipse, its ostensible purpose is to frighten away the animal or monster that is about to devour the heavenly body. The custom has been recorded the world over.[1]

Lévi-Strauss mentions China, Burma, India, Malaysia, Dahomey Africa, Canada, Peru, Mexico, Greece, and Rome. Such a mythology of noise in darkness to scare away demons is not an interpretation of his dream, but rather an interesting archaic human reaction to fear at the time of an eclipse when the world seemed to be coming to an end.

Silent Treatment of Nations

If we are a nation of gap fillers, the malicious use of silence can be a gap filler. In a collective sense, we can consider the silent treatment of nations. Diplomatic frigidity, snub, social and political disdain, nonrecognition, and condem/nation are social and cultural variations of the silent treatment. Such

[1]Lévi-Strauss, Claude. *The Raw and the Cooked: Introduction to a Science of Mythology.* New York: Harper & Row, 1969, p. 301.

attitudes treat the other nation as if it did not exist in our eyes. Thus, after a period of frozen relationships, we speak of "recognizing" the other nation as if it were unknown or nonexistent until we end the silent treatment. This method is a way of telling the unwanted, orphaned nation that it will be welcomed back into "the family of nations" once it sees things our way and capitulates.

Silent treatment can be a metaphor that characterizes genocide and ethnic cleansing, the Holocaust, massacres, and the Reign of Terror in the USSR under Stalin. Masses of people were rendered silent, and in that sense, this is the silent treatment. There is an unprecedented urgency to recognize and admit that sham, indifference, and euphemisms are deadening noises.

C. G. Jung wrote:

> The alarming pollution of our water supply, the steady increase of radioactivity, and the somber threat of overpopulation with its genocidal tendencies has already led to the widespread though not generally conscious fear which loves noise because it stops the fear from being heard. Noise is welcome because it drowns out the inner instinctual warnings. Fear loves noisy company and pandemonium to scare away the demons.[1]

---

[1]Jung, C.G., *Letters,* Vol. 2. Edited by Gerhard Adler. Princeton, N.J.: Princeton University Press, 1975, p. 389 (Letter, September 1957).

2

The Nature of Silence

The wind blows where it chooses, and you hear the sound
of it, but you do not know where it comes from or where it
goes. So it is with everyone who is born of the spirit.

John 3:8

In the Arctic, when the wind is not blowing, you can hear
footsteps in the snow three miles away. The Inuit orient
themselves even in blinding snow by reading the wind. I asked
my friend Edmund Carpenter, anthropologist and Arctic
explorer, "What is silence?" He wrote:

We treat silence as we would treat empty coffers, something without value, like a student without knowledge.
Filling gaps is almost a mark of Western Culture. I have
been told that silence is simply a juncture or a substitute
for a phoneme – meaning speech or a unit of sound in a
language that cannot be analyzed into smaller linear units,
and can distinguish one word from another.[1]

He added that in the Eskimo-Aleut language, a single word
can be a short poem; thus, it would contain many words and
spaces.

We use the word "silence" as a name to be defined. What

[1]Carpenter, Edmund. Personal communication.

we name is not silence, but it is what we call silence. We choose a name for a newborn baby. Once named, the name and the baby become the same. It is as if we pulled the name out of a magician's hat, and presto – the child becomes the name. Carpenter tells me that the Eskimo-Aleut language does not name things that already exist, but that naming brings them into being. For example, when a child is named at birth, an old woman stands by while the mother is in labor, calling out all the different eligible names she can think of. The child comes out when its name is called.

The word becomes what it names, child or silence, although it is not. Lewis Carroll explained it all in *Through the Looking Glass*:

> "The name of the song is called 'Haddock's Eyes.'"
> "Oh, that's the name of the song, is it," Alice said, trying to feel interested.
> "No, you don't understand," the Knight said, looking a little vexed. "That's what the name is called. The name really is, 'The Aged, Aged Man.'"
> "Then I ought to have said, 'That's what the song is called,'" Alice corrected herself.
> "No, you oughtn't, that's another thing. The song is called, 'Ways and Means,' but that's only what it's called, you know."[1]

I define silence as "listening." When I speak the word "silence," I am naming it, but the name is not the same as what I call it. Referring to silence as an "it" is incorrect because silence is not a thing, an object, or any substance. The ultimate silence we associate with eternity and death is unnameable and unknowable.

Analysis is not the "talking cure" that Freud called it.[2] It is not even a cure. It is deep, attentive listening. Psychoanalyst

[1]Carroll, Lewis. *Through the Looking Glass: And What Alice Found There*. New York: Julian Messner, 1982, pp. 226-27.
[2]Freud, Sigmund. *The Complete Psychological Works of Sigmund Freud*, Vol. XI: *Five Lectures on Psychoanalysis*. London: Hogarth Press, 1957, pp. 12, 21.

Theodor Reik called this "listening with the third ear," or learning how one mind speaks to another beyond words and in silence.[1]

My interest in silence stems from my profession of listening as a psychiatrist and analyst. I silently listen to what is said and what is not said – the pauses, silences, and rhythms that give meaning to the stories of my patients' lives.

My listening is made more difficult by an increasing loss of hearing for six years, and dependence on high-tech hearing aids. Being an introvert, humanist, writer, avid reader, and artist, I am in close touch with the inner world of the psyche – a refuge from the other world of the American extroverted way of talking and noisy gap filling.

My interest has always been in dreams – the visual, largely silent messages of the night – especially catastrophic war dreams of posttraumatic stress disorder veterans, hospitalized schizophrenic patients, and prisoners. I have been listening into worlds to which society turns a deaf ear. My great curiosity about such a mysterious realm compelled me to write this book. So … what is silence?

The Oxford English Dictionary defines the word *silence* as the absence of sound or speech. Silence is thereby identified by what it does not contain; that is, what it is not. The dictionary adds that the state of silence may be a condition resulting from muteness, reticence, or taciturnity, and that silence is also used allusively to note the state beyond this life, citing as a material example the Tower of Silence, one of a number of small towers upon the summit of which the Pharisees placed their dead. In music, silence is a rest. Or as Hamlet said, "The rest is silence."[2] My edition of the *Encyclopedia Britannica* has only one entry under *silence*: "See *silencer*."

[1]Reik, Theodor. *Listening with the Third Ear: The Inner Experience of a Psychoanalyst.* 1948.
[2]Shakespeare, William. *Hamlet*. New York: Bantam, 1988.

The word *silence* does not appear in the index of Freud's *Complete Psychological Works*[1] or in Jung's *Collected Works*[2]. Neither of them wrote much on this subject and it is practically ignored in the analytic literature. What is written is rather mundane.

The futility of the definition of something as what it is not can be illustrated by Boyce Richardson's book *People of Terra Nullius*, which describes the legal fiction of defining Canada as a land empty of people that was used to justify seizure of native territory.[3] The sophisticated sham is in pronouncing what is to be what it is not. The same applies to the use of the phrase *Terra Incognito* for Australia and the presumed contiguous Antarctica in the maps drawn by the Alexandrian astronomer, Ptolemy, in the second century.

This idea is also the metaphor of "No Man's Land" in World War II as uninhabitable and belonging to no one. Only the dead inhabited such a place as the ghosts of the departed. The task of living comrades was to remove the corpses – creating the "no man's land," a terrifying place where millions of men were sacrificed to Mars, the god of war.

The Greek god of silence, Harpokratus, sat speechless on a lotus flower. The goddess of silence, Angerone, stood with an uplifted finger touching her lips, suggesting her silence and her suffering. I wonder about the hyperactive, ever-intrusive Harpo Marx, the silent harp-playing Marx brother, who when he wanted to get attention tooted a horn he carried with him. Was he a Hollywood version of Harpokratus?

Eric Maria Remarque (the German soldier who penned *All Quiet on the Western Front*, describing trench warfare, "No Man's Land," and the unbearable noise of shells and explosives) wrote:

[1]Freud, Sigmund. *The Complete Psychological Works of Sigmund Freud*, Standard Ed.: Vols. I-XXIV. London: Hogarth Press, 1974.
[2]Jung. C. G. *Collected Works*, Vols. 1-20. Princeton, N.J.: Princeton University Press, 1979.
[3]Richardson, Boyce. *People of Terra Nullius: Betrayal and Rebirth in Aboriginal Canada*. Seattle: University of Washington Press, 1993.

It is strange that all the memories that come have these two qualities: They are always calm, that is predominant in them; and even if they are not really calm, they become so. They are soundless apparitions that speak to me, with looks and gestures, silently, without any word – and it is the alarm of their silence that forces me to lay hold of my sleeve and my rifle, lest I should abandon myself to the liberation and allurement in which my body would dilate and gently pass into the still forces that lie behind these things. They are quiet in this way, because quietness is so unattainable for us now. At the front there is no quietness and the curse of the front reaches so far that we never pass beyond it.[1]

Philosophers and Poets

Leaving the subject of definitions, I turn to the words of various philosophers and poets who have written about the nature of silence.

Friedrich Nietzsche wrote:

I admire the courage and wisdom of Socrates in everything he did, said, and did not say. This mocking and enamored monster and pied piper of Athens, who made the most arrogant youths tremble and sob, was not only the wisest talker whoever lived: he was just as great in his silences.[2]

The Swiss philosopher, Max Picard, who wrote a profound book entitled *The World of Silence*, said:

When language ceases, silence begins. But it does not begin BECAUSE silence ceases. The absence of language simply makes the presence of Silence more apparent.

[1]Remarque, Eric Maria. *All Quiet on the Western Front*. Boston: Little Brown, 1929, p. 120.
[2]Kaufmann, Walter (Ed.). "The Gay Science" in *The Portable Nietzsche* by Friedrich Wilhelm Nietzsche. New York: Viking, 1954, pp. 101, 340.

Silence is an autonomous phenomenon. It is therefore not identical with the suspension of language. It is not merely the negative condition that sets in when the positive is removed; it is rather an independent whole, subsisting in and through itself. It is creative, as language is creative, but not in the same degree. ... It is language and not silence that makes man truly human. The word has supremacy over silence.

Silence contains everything within itself. It is not waiting for anything; it's always present in itself and it completely fills the space in which it appears. ... Silence has been banished from the world today. ... All that is left is muteness and emptiness. Silence seems to survive as a mere "structural fault" in the everlasting flow of noise. It is therefore all the more important that the silent images should be preserved in the soul.[1]

Thomas Hood, nineteenth-century English poet, wrote:

There is a silence where hath been no sound;
There is a silence where no sound may be; –
In the cold grave; under the deep, deep sea;
Or in a wide desert where no life is found,
Which hath been mute, and still may sleep profound –
No voice is hushed, no life treads silently,
But clouds and cloudy shadows wander free,
That never spoke, over the idle ground.

But in green ruins, in the desolate walls
Of antique palaces, where man hath been,
Though the dun fox, or wild hyena calls,
And owls, that flit continuously between,
Shriek to the echo, and the low winds moan, –
There the true silence is, self-conscious and alone.[2]

[1]Picard, Max. *The World of Silence*. Washington, D.C.: Regnery Gateway, 1988, pp. 17, 92.
[2]Hood, Thomas. "Silence" sonnet in John Bartlett's *Familiar Quotations*. Boston: Little, Brown, 1940, p. 390.

In the words of T. S. Eliot:

> Against the Word the unstilled world still whirled
> About the centre of the silent Word.[1]

Zen Mondo relates:

> A monk asked Master Seppo, "What is the First Word?"
> The Master was silent. The monk went to another Master,
> Chosho, and told him the story. Chosho said to the monk,
> "You are already the man of the second word."[2]

Indian sage and mystic, Ramana Maharishi, has recorded
his thoughts on silence:

> Silence is ever-speaking; it is the perennial flow of "lan-
> guage." It is interrupted by speaking; for words obstruct
> this mute language. Lectures may entertain individuals for
> hours without improving them. Silence, on the other hand,
> is permanent and benefits the whole of humanity. ... By
> silence eloquence is meant. Oral lectures are not so elo-
> quent as silence. Silence is unceasing eloquence. It is the
> best language. This is a state where words cease and
> silence prevails.[3]

The origin of Zen is said to have begun with Buddha's
Flower Sermon:

> On this occasion, he held up a flower to a gathering of
> disciples without saying a word. Only Kasyapa understood
> him.[4]

[1]Eliot, T. S. "Ash-Wednesday" in *T. S. Eliot: Selected Poems*. New York:
Harcourt, Brace and World, 1964, (V), p. 90.

[2]Zen Mondo in Zenkei Shibayama's *A Flower Does Not Talk*. Rutland,
Vermont: Charles E. Tuttle, 1972, p. 17.

[3]Maharishi, Ramana. *Silence and Solitude: The Spiritual Teaching of Ramana
Maharishi*. Boston: Shambhala, 1988, p. 48.

[4]Jung, C. G. Foreword to D. T. Suzuki's *An Introduction to Zen Buddhism*.
New York: Grove Press, 1964, pp. 9-29.

Johann Wolfgang Goethe set down his ideas in *Faust*:

> 'Tis writ, "In the beginning was the word."
> I pause, to wonder what is here inferred.
> The "Word" I cannot set supremely high:
> A new translation I will try.
> I read, if by the spirit I am taught,
> This sense: "In the beginning was the Thought."
> The opening I need to weigh again,
> Or sense may suffer from a hasty pen.
> Does thought create, and work, and rule the hour?
> 'Twer best: "In the beginning was the Power."
> Yet, while the pen is urged with willing figures,
> The spirit comes to guide me in my need,
> I write, "In the beginning was the deed."[1]

Goethe's intention was to detract from the value of the word, and to emphasize that the word was not there in the beginning, but that action was. Word came at the end of development, crowning the deed.[2]

Goethe once considered a vow of silence. He said, "We should talk less, and draw more. Personally, I would like to renounce speech and, like organic nature, communicate everything in sketches."[3]

Pulitzer Prize-winning novelist, Isaac Bashevis Singer, has commented:

> A man may sit for hours and talk about what he thinks. But what he really is, you can best judge by what he does. This is the real heresy in the psychoanalysis of our time when everything is measured by your thoughts and by your moods.

[1]Goethe, Johann Wolfgang. *Faust* (1808). *Harvard Classics*, Vol. 19. New York: P. F. Collier & Son, 1909.
[2]Redner, Harry. *In the Beginning Was the Deed: Reflections on the Passage of Faust*. Berkeley: University of California Press, 1982.
[3]Goethe. Source unknown.

When you read the Bible, it never tells you what a man thought. It always says what he did. ... I myself would never begin a story with, say, "Mr. So-and-so was sitting and thinking." I would rather describe how he looked, what he did and what he said. I would rather give a situation than list his broodings.[1]

Meister Eckhart (1260-1328), German mystic and theologian, transcribed his thoughts:

Out of silence, a secret word was spoken to me. "Ah, sir! – What is this silence and where is that word to be spoken?" We shall say, as I have heretofore, [it is spoken] in the purest element of the soul, in the soul's most exalted place, in the core, yes, the essence of the soul. The central silence is there, where no creature may enter, nor any idea, and there the soul neither thinks nor acts nor entertains any idea, either in itself or of anything else. ... In that core is the central silence, the pure peace, and abode of the heavenly birth, the place for this event: the utterance of God's word.[2]

In the words of Kahlil Gibran:

Ay, you shall be together even in the silent memory of God,
But let there be spaces in your togetherness,
And let the winds of the heaven dance between you ...
For the pillars of the temple stand apart,
And the oak tree and the cypress grow not in each other's shadow.[3]

My soul gave me good counsel, teaching me to listen to the voices not produced by tongues, nor shouted from throats.

[1]Singer, Isaac Bashevis, with Richard Burgin. *Conversations with Isaac Bashevis Singer*. New York: Straus and Giroux, 1985, p. 53.
[2]Eckhart, Meister. (Translated by R. B. Blakney.) New York: Harper & Row, 1941, pp. 96, 97.
[3]Gibran, Kahlil. *The Prophet*. New York: Knopf, 1958, p. 15.

Before my soul taught me, my ears were weary and ailing, and I was conscious only of uproar and discord. Now I sip at silence and listen to its inwardness that chants sounds of the eons, reciting praises of the sky, announcing the mysteries of the unseen.[1]

Pierre Lacout, a Catholic priest of the Carmelite order with the vow of silence, has written a book called *God Is Silence* in which he gives the name Silence to what others would prefer to call The Word. Lacout offers a daily prayer:

Our Father who art in heaven, hallowed be Thy name; Thy kingdom come; Thy will be done on earth as it is in heaven; give us this day our daily silence.[2]

It is one thing to define the word "silence"; it is another to try to explain the nature of silence. It is like the word love. Lovers know that in order to tell the other about their feelings, they have to speak the word "love." The feeling is not defined by the word. One just knows that there is no other word or sound.

The poet, José Ortega y Gasset, wrote:

Lovers understand that in order to communicate their feeling to each other they have to speak these words [my love] or others of the same tenor. They do not understand why their feeling called love, is spoken or expressed by "love" and not by any other sound. Between their personal intention to speak out their feeling and the act of enunciating and producing a certain sound, there is no intelligible connection. If lovers perform this act of enunciation, it is because they have heard that it is done when two people love each other, but not for any reason that we find in the word "love." [3]

[1]Gibran, Kahlil. *The Vision: Reflections on the Way of the Soul*. Ashland, Oregon: White Cloud Press, 1994, p. 98.
[2]Lacout, Pierre. *God Is Silence*. London: Friends Home Service Committee, 1969, p. 3.

It is said that God is love but neither God nor love can be defined. "God is love" expresses a numinous religious experience.

While writing this book, I had a dream from which I woke up in the morning saying half-aloud to myself, "I dreamed that I saw a brilliant intrusion into the nature of silence." In the dream, I was searching for something that was lost when a voice called out to me, "Your quest for silence is in the Caribbean. It is located just east of the Yucatán in the Gulf of Mexico. In the place is the Center of Thought."

I instantly realized that this was an important dream from my unconscious which had been searching in depth for Silence and had located its center – essence or core, to use Meister Eckhart's idea. I lay quietly in bed pondering the meaning of the dream revelation. Specific word sounds from an invisible source had commanded and instructed me as to where I could find Silence. I associate the Gulf of Mexico east of Yucatán with the location of the lost continent of Atlantis that had sunk into the sea. The dream specifically said that "I saw" a brilliant intrusion into the nature of silence. It was an insight deep into the mythology of the collective unconscious which is, since the sea is the nature of silence, a place of pilgrimage.

[3]Ortega y Gasset, José. *Man and People*. New York: W. W. Norton, 1957, pp. 223-24.

3

Pandemonium and Silence

This morning I heard the radio announcer on Austin's KLBJ station say, "It's so foggy today that you actually have to watch where you are driving."

Four years ago, a small grey and white kitten appeared in our garden. Starving and abandoned, he would not leave. When I walked on the path, he too walked slowly, directly in front of my feet. His silent, persistent, graceful manner was beguiling and arresting. He would do the same when my wife, Jane, walked the path. This situation continued for two days. I decided to keep him. With food and love, he was transformed into a large, beautiful, affectionate cat who stays with me constantly. Jane named him "Mitten" because of his four white paws, and I call him "Mitten-Kitten."

Every morning before breakfast, I take a half-hour walk around our three acres. Mitten walks in front of me at a distance of several feet. Mitten does what I ask him to do – after a fashion and with an independent air. When I am writing or painting, he sits at my feet or in his chair in my greenhouse. This silent peaceful cat fills an animal void in my life.

It was still dark this morning when Mitten and I took our walk. He led with stealthy steps by sensing where I was going. Mitten's ears would turn backward and cup the sounds of my steps. With the first rays of the morning sun, I stopped and looked around. Suddenly a shrieking noise shot overhead – a low-flying military jet. As the sound whined away, the three quartz guardlights in the oak trees blinked off automatically in response to the sun. Just over the wooden fence, I saw a light turn on in our neighbor's house. I felt as if Mitten's and my old routine had been suddenly shattered with the sound of the fighter jet.

New sounds seemed to erupt – the noise of Interstate Highway 35 a mile to the south. I usually don't hear the cars and trucks there, like an endlessly racing heart. Had the sound emerged to fill the quiet space left by the fading airplane, or was it a reversal of my selective auditory attention?

The groaning noise of the highway has been growing louder ever since it became the principal north-south NAFTA (North American Free Trade Agreement) highway from Mexico through Texas.

The racket reminded me of the horrendous noise on IH-35 during Operation Desert Storm in the Gulf War when it was the main artery to carry tanks, armored vehicles, cannons, ammunition, and soldiers from Fort Hood at Killeen, Texas, the largest armored military base in the world. Killeen is seventeen miles away from our peaceful country home in the charming rural village of Salado – population three thousand. Salado is growing. There were four hundred people and no traffic when we moved here in 1970. The noise is moving in.

Mitten and I followed the path as it circled the clusters of trees inside our fenced property. Mitten showed no sign of reaction to the noises that were distressing me. I surmised that he heard everything that I did but focused his instinctual superacute hearing along the ground, allured by the sounds of small animals and insects inaudible to me.

In a flash, Mitten bolted from the path and disappeared into the brush. After a while, when I was finishing my walk, I came to the back door of my greenhouse above which is mounted an old sunbleached steer's skull with big horns. Mitten was waiting for me. At my feet, I saw a small circle of limestones that Jane has arranged around a thin stem of a plant, to warn me not to walk on it. If I step on my cat, he will let me know; if I step on a flower stem, it will die. I walked into the greenhouse and next to the window saw the framed Zen poem that I had lettered and painted in watercolors. It said:

> Silently a flower blooms,
> In silence it falls away;
> Yet here now, at this moment,
> at this place,
> The whole of the flower,
> the whole of
> the world is blooming.
> This is the talk of the flower,
> the truth of the blossom;
> The glory of eternal life
> is fully shining here.[1]

Pandemonium (Greek for "all the demons") was described by John Milton in *Paradise Lost* as the principal city of hell characterized by lawless tumult and unrestrained, quintessential noise. The fallen angels forged Pandemonium as the Palace of All the Demons from Metals of Hell.[2] *Paradise Lost* symbolically depicts the Industrial Revolution in Great Britain with its brutalizing noise and filthy factories. "Among these flaming, smoky, clanging [ironworks] I beheld the remains of what had once been happy farmhouses, now ruined and deserted."[3]

Thomas Carlyle warns "... and in this hag-ridden dream, mistake God's fair living world for a pallid, vacant Hades and extinct Pandemonium."[4] The dictionary enlarges Milton's original Pandemonium as also being a place of vice and

---

[1]Zenkei Shibayami (Nanzenji Monastery, Kyoto, Japan). *A Flower Does Not Talk: Zen Essays*. Rutland, Vermont: Charles E. Tuttle, 1972.

[2]Milton, John. *Paradise Lost:* Harvard Classics, Vol. 4. New York: P.F. Collier, 1909.

[3]Jenning, Humphrey. *Pandemonium 1660-1896: The Coming of the Machine as Seen by Contemporary Observers*. New York: Free Press, 1985.

[4]Carlyle, Thomas. *Sartor Resartus*. New York: Dutton, 1973, (Book II, Chapter iii: "Pedagogy"), p. 87.

wickedness, a gathering of wild lawless violence, confusion, and uproar.

America today writhes with noise. On the street, people blast boom boxes. Cars cruise with windows down and radios blaring. People revel in vociferous insults and crude gansta rap. Politicians argue with self-righteous contention. Civility is on its way out. TV audiences glue themselves to the tube watching men, women, and children being blown up, shot, and slaughtered, with violence glorified. Everything can at anytime explode into roaring fireballs. Our acoustic space bang-crashes with noisy, wildly clever commercials.

In a letter to Karl Otlinger, professor of law at the University of Zurich and founder of an association to combat noise, Jung wrote:

> I personally detest noise and flee from it whenever and wherever possible, because it not only disturbs the concentration needed for my work, but forces me to the additional psychic effort of shutting it out. Noise is certainly one of the evils of our time, though perhaps the most intrusive, the others are the gramophone, the radio, and now the blight of the television.[1]

As a rule, normal introverted people thrive on quiet and solitude. Highly introverted people, schizoid individuals, or people with some forms of schizophrenia, seek silence as sanctuary from an intolerable, hostile, outer world and tormenting hallucinations and delusions in the inner world. By patiently listening to individuals struggling to find silence or some place as sanctuary, we will learn more about the inherent human search for inner silence, quiet, and peace.

---

[1]Jung, Carl. *Letters*, Vol. 2, edited by Gerhard Adler. Princeton, N.J.: Princeton University Press, 1975, pp. 388-89.

A Patient Seeks Sanctuary in Silence

A shy, withdrawn, twenty-year-old woman consulted me. She was pretty, with a sylphlike presence that seemed to radiate silence. The young woman said, "I have to talk to someone who will understand my fears."

I will call her Helen. She was a university student happily married to an introverted, shy, caring husband. She spoke hesitantly, clearly, and softly. We met for an hour once a week working with her pervasive anxieties and fears. After we had worked for several months, Helen was notably less tense and fearful. I told her that I was writing a book about silence and I would be very interested in her thoughts about that subject. I said, "Tell me about silence." She responded immediately:

Helen: "I feel protected, like I am part of things, but to be part of things is threatening. If I don't speak, I'm not part, and outside I walk. Nobody can touch me if I don't say anything."

Harry: "How young were you when you remembered first doing that?"

Helen: "Very young. Before first grade, like preschool. When I was four years old, I wanted to have friends. I didn't have any brothers or sisters.

"I can't think when there is noise like someone talking – at least, not to me. It's like being in a car and wanting to speak. I can't have the music on, or at home have the TV on. Silence is where I live. I remember in fourth grade, the rooms were partitioned with pull curtains. All the curtains were open and we were all doing something. In my mind, it was silent because nobody was talking to me. I spoke to my mind what everyone out there ought to hear – to communicate, to hear me. I screamed in my head and nobody answered.

"It's kind of like silence where I live. We have a very quiet house. Nobody ever yells or screams or does a lot of talking. I don't have the TV or radio on very often. Very quiet. So I just have to sit there and listen, and I formulate in my mind all the things I would like to say. It is like the silence is here [gestures] over my mouth. But I can still hear what they are saying.

Sometimes like I am working on some stuff back in here [gestures to the back of her head] that I would say if I could. It is frustrating because silence is hard to break out of.

"Silence is the place where my mind lives. When I am interacting with people, I have come through somewhere else, but when there is no noise there, when there is silence, that's when I was near where my mind really was."

A few weeks later, Helen said she was doing better and thought that we had accomplished all that was necessary. Her basic problem had not changed but she felt more comfortable with it. Helen said she was pleased that we had audiotaped a session and she had learned from listening to it.

Having listened to Helen's fears, and seen more balance between her inner and outer worlds, I felt that pursuing her psychotherapy deeper or longer would be counterproductive. I did not say that to her, but agreed with her that we could stop now and she could come back to see me later if she wished. I felt that she had told me all she wanted to about her secret world of silence.

The Off-and-On Phenomena

Listening to speech, we hear alternate sounds and silences. It is the silent pauses between words and thoughts that give speech its rhythm, from musical to raucous. Ordinary dialogue flows in a linear temporal sequence. A subjective conversation can be plotted objectively by a series of symbols (standing for words) and intervening spaces like a musical score.

Music, however, permeates imaginary space in both a lineal and three-dimensional way. It has a beginning and an end. Symphonies often build to great crescendos followed by crashing silence. The abrupt silence is a sobering nonsound commentary on what has just transpired. It is the off-and-on nature of notes and rest symbols for designated lengths of silence that creates the musical score.

Edmund Burke, eighteenth-century English author and statesman, wrote:

> A sudden beginning or cessation of sound in any consider-able force has great power. ... Few things are more awful than the striking of a great clock when the silence of the night prevents the attention from being too dissipated. The same can be said for the single stroke of a drum, repeated with pauses; and of successive firings of a cannon at a distance.[1]

When I was a small child in the 1920s, my father gave me a crystal radio set that I could hold in the palm of my hand. By scratching a small crystal with a fine-pointed wire, I heard through earphones sounds miraculously plucked from the air. People were talking and music was playing in my head. To a child, the mechanism was unbelievably simple. Imagine all those sounds floating around in space that we could not hear.

I was also intrigued with the telegraphic key at the small local railroad station. The stationmaster would tap out messages to the other stations in Morse code of dots and dashes separated by silences. It had an hypnotic effect as I imagined these sounds traveling over the telegraph wires alongside the tracks. This experience is a classical example of lineal messages. I learned the Morse code as a Boy Scout so I could signal SOS by telegraph keys, waving flags, or blinking lights.

The contrasting opposites of speech and silence in a non-linear manner can be illustrated by the pantomime (etymological meaning: "a dumb show") of the old *commedia dell'arte*, where the sweethearts, Harlequin and Columbine, never spoke and Pantalone, Harlequin's father, never stopped talking. Harlequin was a childlike amorous wit who wore a catlike mask and motley-colored clothes, and carried a bat or wooden sword. He was the ancestor of slapstick comedy – Harpo and Harpokratus again.

---

[1]Burke, Edmund. "Suddenness" in *On the Sublime and Beautiful:* Harvard Classics, Vol. 24. New York: P. F. Collier and Son, 1909, p. 73.

When I was four years old and lived in New Orleans, Louisiana, my parents brought me and my six-year-old sister to Atlanta to visit our wealthy uncle who lived in a grand white mansion. He was a kind old southern gentleman who struck awe. One afternoon he took me, my sister, and our parents for a ride in his black limousine driven by a handsome black chauffeur. A glass partition, which rolled up and down, stood closed between the front and back seats. My uncle spoke to the chauffeur through a tube with a horn at the end of it. A crystal flower vase with a flower was positioned quietly in the car.

My sister and I sat on the two jump seats that folded into the rear of the front seat facing the adults in the back. My uncle talked all the time while my parents listened reverentially. Suddenly, he stopped speaking for what seemed to me a long time. When I could no longer endure it, I spoke my first words in a firm voice, "Speak, man, speak!"

To my embarrassment, mother, father, and sister laughed, but the white-haired old man with a goatee immediately began talking just to me. We had a charming conversation while the others were quiet. This little episode made me famous with my father, who told the story over and over again.

Today, my professional role is to get people to speak to me so that I can listen to them. Our conversations fascinate me. The dialogue is civil and connected, now that I am the bald white-haired man whom they generally treat well. The nature of our speech and silence is healing, partly because it is so strikingly different from the gap-filling, noisy, bossy, interrupting talk-show mentality in which we live.

The dialogue I strive for is more like that of the early native Americans in treaty conversations. Having spoken their piece, the Indians would silently listen without interruption to the talking white men, expecting them to listen in the same manner. This pattern is strikingly evident in transcriptions of early negotiations.

To enter this kind of exchange in a contrived manner or façade, however, is not total listening but rather a clever miming deception. At first, the Indians believed the white man as explained in the history of the Lewis and Clark Expedition, but they were fed lies and trickery in a grand manner by those speaking for the Indians' new unknown, benevolent Great Father in Washington. The Indians' attentiveness was enticed by gifts of whisky, beads, guns, bullets, and powder.

Max Picard describes the nature of genuine listening:

> Listening is possible only when there is silence in man: Listening and silence go together. Instead of truly speaking to others today we are all waiting to unload onto others the words that have collected inside us. Speech has become a purely animal execrative function.[1]

Execrative means cursing, denouncing, detesting, and passionate condemnation – in short, the rhetoric of the powerful to the lesser people. You can hear and see this type of speech on television in the hostile debates and arguments in Congress. Such speaking is a form of noise meant for uncritical consumption by the good folks back home, and woe to those who would try to silence the voices of power. These voices are for sale by those who make large financial contributions. The speaking time is either dished out in limited bites ("I yielded my last minute to …") or in the greatest gap-filling exercise known to which no one listens: the filibuster, with its portentous marathon of words. The grand show and posture is noticeable by the empty seats in the chamber when congressional representatives pontificate for television.

It takes a woman of extraordinary intellect and wit to outmaneuver the powerful congressional who claim that they own time. Elspeth Rostow, professor of American studies at the University of Texas at Austin, was called with a group of humanists to testify in the debate on the funding of the National Endowment for the Humanities.

She recalls:

---

[1] Picard, *World of Silence*, p. 177.

Senator Claiborne Pell was the chairman of the committee. It was on a Friday. I think he wanted to get back to
Rhode Island and go sailing. In any case he got impatient
with us and asked us to define "humanities" in one sentence. The president of [Georgetown University] started,
but a minefield developed when Pell cut him short. "Sorry,
Father. That's more than one sentence. Next." So I started
my definition of the humanities and saw the same minefield ahead, and so I said, "semicolon," and that broke up
the audience. Pell looked at me angrily, but I was able to
finish my definition.[1]

It is convenient to speak of the Off-and-On Phenomenon of
speech, dividing it into separate categories of words and
silence. That is an artificial construct, however, derived from
scientific thinking. It is the purpose of my book to show that
silence is pervasive, everywhere, always, and has no boundaries. Onto this endless sea of silence, words are imposed. This
silence is often alluded to in spiritual terms. The silence to
which I now refer is not the silence of rhetoric, grammar, or
theology, but rather the ultimate silence of limitless time-
space – in which there is only one event, as in quantum
physics.

Danah Zohar in her book, *On the Quantum Self*, speaks of
quantum physics, which is essentially both wavelike and
particle-like simultaneously:

There is no space between separate objects such as we
normally think of them, and the whole notion of "separate"
has no foundation in reality. How do we talk about events,
or relationships, if we must give up all talk of time and
never say that one thing causes another to happen?
Quanta listening is a term used to mean equality in shared
space. Segments of speech delivered and heard according
to the definition of quanta, refer to a dialogue of discreet

---

[1]Seale, Avrel. "Sipping Tea with Elspeth Rostow" in *Alcalde*, January 1996,
Vol. 84, No. 3.

uninterrupted speech by one person followed by the other, during which time the other listens in silence.[1]

Einstein wrote in a letter to Jacques Hadamord:

The words or language, as they are written or spoken, do not seem to play any role in my mechanism of thought. The psychical entities which seem to serve as elements of thought are certain signs and more or less clear images which can be voluntarily reproduced or combined. ... The essential feature in productive thought [is] before any connection with logical construction in words of any other kinds of signs which can be communicated to others.[2]

This morning I went for a swim before I went to my greenhouse to write. The sky was a muted grey and I felt as if I were under a great opaque dome. All around the periphery at the horizon, under a rim of bright grey, the sky became black. A storm was hanging all around me. As I was swimming on my back, I saw overhead three giant birds flying south. When I got home, I wrote down my fleeting thoughts:

"For some reason I do not understand, I am hearing quiet, melodious music and indistinct poetry being read. I say the words laughter and silence and then ask myself, 'What has laughter to do with silence?' In response, I hear the pleasant laughter of someone who was listening. The laughter seemed to float through the air like the giant birds flying south in the grey sky before the storm. The storm? This morning is on the threshold of noise like laughter gone wild. At this moment, the sky is split by a bolt of lightning, followed by the shattering boom of thunder and a downpour of rain.

[1]Zohar, Danah, in collaboration with I. N. Marshall. *The Quantum Self: Human Nature and Consciousness Defined by the New Physics*. New York: Morrow, 1990, p. 25.
[2]Ghiselin, Brewster (Ed.). *The Creative Process: A Symposium*. New York: New American Library, 1952, pp. 43-44.

"I was reminded of the boisterous roaring laughter of a pompous doctor when he came to work every morning and settled down at his power desk. His laugh was not like natural thunder but like that of a cock-a-doodle-do, announcing Senator Foghorn's arrival. It was not a good belly laugh but rather a series of explosions every day, saying, 'I am here! Attila the Hun has arrived! The big honcho, the Great Boss Eagle has landed!' I hated the noise and the man. It was silence followed by pandemonium.

"I walk down into the house for breakfast. It is still raining heavily, and there is lightning and thunder. Jane is putting food on the table. I think how pretty she is, at seventy-two radiating peace, contentment, and simple happiness. We eat breakfast in total silence. We can hear the sound of raindrops hitting something. The sound of the rain will be impressive on the tin roof of my greenhouse when I go back up there to write again on my silence book."

I have been thinking of a vacuum, which theoretically is a space without matter. We call it empty space with nothing in it. Practically, a vacuum is a region of space in which atmospheric pressure has been reduced as much as possible with pumping systems, or as much as is necessary to prevent the influence of atmosphere on processes being carried out within the space. I think it would approximate an artificially bounded silent space.

It is said that Nature abhors a vacuum. The vacuum can be used as a model for the conventional definition of silence: "Space devoid of sound." Americans experience silence as a vacuum, an artificial gap into which they are anxiously sucked. It is like our filling-up compulsion. Inside, there is nothing.

Try to imagine nothing: Imagining presupposes an image. Americans cannot imagine silence. A mystic, however, can empty his mind, and then there is nothing in it to distract his contemplation.

A hole is an empty space. One of my patients, whom I will call Kate, told me that at her first meeting with her previous therapist, he had instructed her to "close your eyes and imagine that you are falling down into a deep hole. Tell me what you see." This suggestion surprised Kate, but she obeyed. When she opened her eyes, Kate said, "When I reached bottom, I found myself in a hexagonal space where there were eight closed large oak doors."

She was startled and intrigued by her unusual vision. She waited for the doctor to say something. He sat watching her, not saying a word – silent treatment again. She felt angry and betrayed, and said to herself, "Goddamn you! What did you ask me to do that for?" It went through her mind that she had acquiesced to a man's command to close her eyes and do something and was then deserted and ignored.

Kate was frightened by him, yet had to be a "good person and swallow my anger." The doctor was totally insensitive to what had happened and continued to ask her questions as if nothing had happened. He gave her an appointment for a second meeting the next week. Two days later, she called and canceled it. Kate told the story to a friend of hers, who advised her to call me for an appointment.

Kate was a divorced, highly intelligent, attractive woman who expressed contempt for the therapist who had invited her to fall into a deep space and, when she told him what she saw, turned to stone silence. It was obvious from her description and feelings that her conscious vision in the hole held profound symbolic meaning. The doctor has gotten in over his head, so he went on in his routine way during the initial interview.

I did not try to analyze the hexagonal space with its eight closed oak doors because I did not want to waste time dealing with a dumb doctor's ignorance. I listened, acknowledged her justified anger, and remained silent about her misadventure.

It was like Samuel Beckett's play, *Theater of Silence*. His characters are trapped, speech is pointless, and they stare at the audience and say nothing. The existentialist Theater of the Absurd has its psychological predisposing terrifying forces. It is worth noting that in an interview in the *New York Times*,

Samuel Beckett is reported as saying that "the only consistency of thought or form he once claimed to see in his work was that of the ceaseless screaming of a man he heard in hospital dying of throat cancer."[1]

My Most Daunting Experience

My wife and I took the ship *Renaissance* on a cruise of the Greek Isles to celebrate our fiftieth wedding anniversary. For many years, I had experienced intermittent chest pain with exertion. A tablet of nitroglycerin medication placed under my tongue would control the anginal pain, and then I could walk. During the last days of the cruise, however, the medication gave no relief.

As the passengers from the ship walked through the village streets, I slowly began to lag far behind. Not wanting to alarm Jane, I did not tell her the severity of my pain. Consequently, she kept egging me on to walk faster and keep up with the group. On the last day of the cruise, on the Island of Santorini, my chest pain worsened and continued even when I did not move. We had one full day left in Athens, where we would get our flight home.

It was a beastly hot July afternoon, and foolishly I decided to visit a crowded shopping area alone. My pace was agonizingly slow and interrupted by sitting at every available bench. Before I returned to the hotel, I bought small alabaster statuettes of Hippocrates, Plato, Aristotle, and Athena. When I put the larger Hippocrates in the bundle, I suddenly realized that I was in serious trouble. Not seeing a taxi, I got into a waiting bus that would go by the hotel. A few blocks before the hotel, I saw the large Athens Cardiovascular Hospital but would not ask the driver to stop. I was determined to get back to the United States and call my doctor at the Mayo Clinic. I

---

[1]Nightingale, Benedict. *New York Times*, "Theater," February 26, 1984.

knew that if I told the tour people of my state, they would not let me travel.

Being a doctor, I made my own decision. There is a saying that the doctor who has himself for his physician has a fool for a doctor. I was being foolhardy (read fool*hearty*). Since I had not had a heart attack with crushing chest pain, sharp pain radiating down my left arm, perspiration, and panic, I decided that there was an interval of time before those symptoms would happen and I would take the chance of getting home before that occurred. I did not allow myself to think that my plan might jeopardize the flight, but I also knew that my salvation was to get to the Mayo Clinic. Having trained at Mayo, and been on the permanent consultation staff, I was convinced that it was the best place in the world. I was counting on prayer, luck, and skill.

When I reached our hotel room in Athens and lay down on the bed, I could not confide my great apprehension to Jane. She scolded me for taking a walk in the hot afternoon all by myself. The pain was constant but not unbearable.

In the morning, we flew on Lufthansa Air Lines from Athens to Frankfurt, where we were to change to a plane that went to the United States. Horrors: I was told by the clerk at the desk that all the reservations for our group to America had been canceled in error. The clerk told me the plane was full, but to stand by. I dreaded being left in Frankfurt. With great effort at meditation, I remained calm, and by a twist of fate, just as the plane was being boarded, a voice on the loud-speaker called our names and said we were on the plane. Not everyone in our group got on. There was great consternation in the group.

When we were in Texas, I telephoned my doctor at Roches-ter, Minnesota (Philip Brown), and told him the situation. His response was, "Harry, I want you to report in at St. Mary's Hospital tomorrow morning." As we sat in our taxi going from the airport, the magnificent Mayo Clinic buildings loomed ahead. Carried by wheelchair into the emergency area of St. Mary's Hospital, I felt, "At last, home and safe."

I was a medical student in 1937 when I first went to St. Mary's Hospital on a summer pathology clerkship. Later, I was a fellow and then on the staff. Mayo had been an inspiration to me since 1933, when my father had arranged a special visit just for me with both Doctors Will and Charlie Mayo. The Mayo spirit never left me. I breathed it again that day at St. Mary's when I was met by the cardiovascular surgical team and a courteous clerk doing the necessary paperwork.

When I was in my room, the doctors began the diagnostic studies and treatment. Efficient and civil, nurses and technicians went about their tasks – X-rays, blood tests, electrocardiogram, echocardiogram. My cardiac surgeon began talking to me about open heart surgery, but said we first needed an angiogram to study the level of closure of my coronary arteries. In the evening, this procedure was performed by inserting a small catheter into the vein through an incision in my groin. A catheter was threaded through the blood vessels into my heart as medical personnel followed it on the fluoroscope screen. They injected opaque dyes into my coronary arteries, showing that all three were 90-95 percent closed.

Then, while I was still on the examination table, something went wrong. My pulse must have stopped, because they were trying to get it. A nurse said something I did not hear, and there was a whirlwind of activity around me. More doctors and nurses were coming into the room. I felt dizzy and faint and was floating away. Something serious had happened, but I did not seem to care. In a detached, vague way I was wondering if my heart had stopped beating or if I were dying. Then I felt peaceful, and everything became quiet. The doctors were injecting medications into my arms, and fluid ran into the veins in my arms from hanging containers. After a period, I floated back into the space I had left. My surgeon told me that he was scheduling emergency triple bypass surgery first thing in the morning.

It must have been approaching midnight when I was wheeled back to my room on a gurney, given an injection of a sedative, and more needles with tubes inserted into the veins of my hands and arms. There was a hanging garden of plastic bags suspended from steel posts. I watched the fluid drip through plastic tubes until I fell asleep.

I suddenly woke up startled. My leg felt wet. By the nightlight in my room, I saw blood pouring out of the groin wound through which the catheter had been inserted. Where was the catheter? Had I pulled it out? I pressed the call button and a nurse appeared at my door almost at once. She put a compress bandage over the wound, and called the surgical resident. He came running in and pressed very hard on the compress bandage with one hand over the other, and both elbows stiff. He held this arduous position for about forty-five minutes until the danger of bleeding had passed.

The surgery did not happen the first thing in the morning. It was early afternoon before an attendant arrived with a gurney to take me to surgery. The anesthetist injected the anesthesia and asked me to count. After four or five, I lost track while sinking into a deep bright space, surrounded by strange echoing sounds. Then I disappeared into a scintillating cascade of muted colors.

It has always been a sensational experience when I wake up out of the void of general anesthesia. It seems that just seconds ago I was put to sleep. In this case, it turned out that I had been unconscious on the operating table for five hours. Slowly I realized where I was, but remained confused about the fact that whatever had happened was all over. Then I realized that the surgery was over. Someone was talking to me. Hubbub, mechanical noises, beeping monitors – machines everywhere were clinking and plinking. Now I was in the intensive care unit. People emerged as if out of a mist, like larvae out of cocoons. With all the muted sounds and voices, there was a surreal quality of silence eating time.

I think I am intact. That is reassuring. I survived. A nurse is busy doing something with my arms and legs, which are tied to retaining bars on each side of the bed. I am the center of a spider web of tubes, drains, and suspended dripping fluid bottles. In an instant, I see myself like an automobile suspended on a rack getting a Quick Lube.

White blurs of people move quickly here and there. After a while, I am aware that Jane has come into the unit and is sitting in a chair on my left side. She is smiling and asks, "How is my baby?" It was shocking to realize that I was mute. I feel sharp pain in my throat and see what looks like a stove pipe sticking out of my mouth. It dawns on me that this is an endotracheal breathing tube that the surgeon had put down my trachea to keep my airway open. My surgeon had told me that he would insert an endotracheal tube, but did not remind me that since it passed through my larynx between the vocal cords, I would not be able to talk. Intellectually I knew this, but I had buried the thought that it would happen to me. It would have been wise for the anesthesiologist or surgeon to have reminded me of this situation before the surgery.

To be unable to speak a word, to feel a big tube sticking down your throat that you cannot pull out, evokes the fear of being suffocated while in restraints. Moreover, I was physically weak, groggy from medication, and confined in a bizarre space. This entire experience was a torture to me. Throttled, speechless, totally dependent, and in pain with an exhaust pipe stuck down my throat was a dreadful state. It seemed to me that this sorry condition lasted for four days, but Jane told me it was twenty-four hours.

Besides all the tubes going into my arms, legs, and hands, there were several wires connected to my heart that came out of my thorax, and rubber drainage tubes coming out of my chest and abdomen. A nurse told me that my left leg, which felt strange, was encased in a pneumatic tube that electronically breathed in and out to aid circulation because the surgeon had stripped a vein from my left ankle to my left groin. They were finding spare parts – blood vessels to use in the by-pass connections so that blood could flow around the obstructed coronary blood vessels. They also used the inner blood vessel, the mammary artery from my chest wall, as a by-pass connection.

The surgeons had disconnected my heart from its connecting arteries and veins, removed it from my body, and hooked the heart and me back up using mechanical devices to assure the flow of life-giving blood. For the first time in my life, there was no beating heart in my chest, no "lub dub" marking time.

Add to this fact that my state of mind and my brain had been put to sleep with powerful anesthesia. For over three hundred minutes, I had neither brain nor heart sounds. I was artificially alive, and as close to the ultimate silence as any human being can be.

It is a known fact that when a human being is placed in an experimental sensory-deprived environment, such as suspension in an underwater tank or in an anechoic chamber, the only sounds one hears are heartbeats and the brain's crinkling sound. I compare this situation with an unconscious fetus suspended in the amniotic fluid of its mother's uterus, with the normal mother's heartbeat replaced by a mechanical heart.

It is more than a coincidence that, after my open-heart surgery, I had my writing hermitage – the greenhouse – built in the backyard where I would write my book on silence. At my annual check-up at Mayo, I told this to my old friend, Dr. Jeffrey Rome, who had also had open-heart surgery. He replied that after his surgery, he had built a silent retreat on a small island in Lake Superior, accessible only by private boat. No phone. No electricity.

Musical genius, John Cage, wrote a book entitled *Silence* in which he says:

> There is no such thing as silence. Get thee to an anechoic chamber and hear things there, thy nervous system in operation and thy blood in circulation.

When Cage experimented by going into an anechoic room, as silent as is mechanically possible, he heard two sounds: one high which he said was his nervous system, and one low that was his circulation. This experience led him to the conclusion that there is no such thing as silence.

A doctor who practices meditation is quoted as saying:

Although in my case, it doesn't seem to be related to telegraphic impressions. It gets much louder after meditation – indeed, it can be almost deafening at these times, although the paradoxical thing is that, no matter how loud it may seem to be, it never interferes with hearing ordinary sounds – in fact, I suspect that my hearing is unusually acute at these times. When I was a boy, I used to think of it as the "sound of silence."[1]

[1]Cohen, J. M., and Phipps. *The Common Experience*. Los Angeles: Tarcher, 1979, pp. 218-19.

4

Listening

Today one of my patients – a handsome, shy, talented young man – announced at the start of the hour that he had fallen in love since I saw him last week, and was eager to tell me the whole story. It was not only extremely interesting but also a rare event in his life. When he began, I had a strong hunch that I should let him speak without asking any questions or interrupting. An inner voice told me that he would talk the whole hour so both he and I would be listeners, and it would be wrong for me to talk. That was a value judgment. I said to myself, "Harry, just listen. Listen to every word, silence, and metaphor, but keep your mouth shut, except for a nod now and then with 'uhuh' or 'yes.'"

I followed the doctor's orders, and was pleased to listen to the story unfold in its own way. At the end of the hour, I said a few words. When I listen this attentively, I can be certain that whatever I say – if I do not say much – will be appropriate. I compare this role to a solitary naturalist walking along a small rushing creek in a previously unknown place in the forest, noting everything seen and heard.

As a rule, when people say, "I just listened," they mean they listened with a part of their attention focused on the other, and another part on themselves. Real listening is a form of communion of being – never just listening, and never wholly possible. Because it is healing, it is one of the joys of being an analyst. The temptation to make big interpretations and ask penetrating questions in such a normal life crisis is apt to be motivated to assure therapists of their own creativity or brilliance, or an unnecessary justification for being there.

Total listening is silent, compassionate communication. The words are held in the inner dialogue in the listener's mind, being the Great Teacher, as in Socratic terms, the daemonian that sits on your shoulder, speaking just to you.

The above example of listening represents a process desperately needed to counteract the increasingly insensitive gap-filling American jabbering. Sir Laurens van der Post warns us:

> For the highest price men have always paid and still pay for all they acquire, whether of matter or spirit, is a psychological one. Human cultures at their most creative best have tried to ensure that what was bought or earned or sought after was also psychologically or spiritually or, at the very least, aesthetically worth it, and of some abiding value, unconnected with any functional significance of the moment. But all these considerations have tended to vanish from contemporary value, and man is increasingly regarded as output or export fodder, and the reward he earns in the process more and more exclusively calculated in materialistic terms. Behind all this, there seems to me to be betrayal of the most reprehensible kind, subversion of a kind not spun by some subtle Russian with snow on his boots in some unheated basement in the Kremlin, but by the institutions and vocations which Western man has evolved precisely in order to protect himself against this sort of treason. ... [van der Post says that this is] the fourth dimension betrayal by the guardians of his spirit, the churches, priests, doctors and teachers of his day.
>
> I lump them together because they are uniquely charged by life with the task of keeping man and his society whole.[1]

A poem by Thomas Merton:

---

[1]van der Post, Sir Laurens. "The Dreamer that Remains" in *The Rock Rabbit and the Rainbow* edited by Robert Hinshaw. Einsiedeln, Switzerland: Daimon Verlag, 1998, pp. 318-19.

In Silence

Be still
Listen to the stones of the wall
Be silent, they try to speak your

Name.
Listen
To the living walls.
Who are you?
Who
Are you? Whose
Silence are you?[1]

In the late 1960s, Dr. Kenneth Colby, a Freudian training analyst at the San Francisco Psychoanalytic Institute, was reporting research success using a computer program he called DOCTOR to act as a psychotherapist. His program was based on a natural language computer program for nondirective psychotherapy created by Joseph Weizenbaum at the MIT Artificial Intelligence Program in 1966, called ELIZA after Eliza Doolittle in *My Fair Lady* (based on G. B. Shaw's play, *Pygmalion*). Weizenbaum was surprised when people whom he tested were convinced that the machine understood them and requested private consultation with the computer.

It is understandable that almost forty years ago, leaders at the orthodox Freudian Institute did not look kindly on a mechanical psychotherapy with a technician at the controls. Colby, a brilliant teacher and well-liked analyst in the San Francisco Institute, found himself demoted from the role of training analyst to an ordinary psychoanalyst. His research in psychotherapy, however, was welcomed by the Stanford University psychology department. Colby left San Francisco and came to Palo Alto, where I invited him to share my private practice office with me.

[1]Merton, Thomas, *The Seven Storey Mountain*. Boston: Houghton Mifflin, 1984, p. 293.

Subjects (read *patients*) spoke with a nonhuman respondent (read *therapist*) in a box, which could be turned on or off at will. They could silence the therapist if they did not like the response. Obviously, a canned analyst practicing psychotherapy (not psychoanalysis) was *persona non grata* to the practitioners of the art of analysis – which they maintained was a science. Colby was carrying out scientific research to assess patterns of words in therapeutic dialogue.

Philip DeMuth, in an article entitled "Eliza and Her Offspring," summed up the advantages of a computer over a human psychotherapist in a whimsical and insightful manner:

> It is never tired. It does not get impatient or enmeshed in countertransference difficulties. It is not concerned with the fight it had with its wife or husband that morning when it was supposed to be listening to clients, or wishing it was on the golf course. It works twenty-four hours a day for a few cents worth of electricity. And ELIZA doesn't have sex with clients.[1]

Colby continued his research, but Weizenbaum subsequently declared that "computerized psychotherapy is immoral and obscene [because] the computer fails to provide interpersonal respect and understanding."[2]

I had the following dialogue with one of my patients, who was a distinguished professor:

> *Harry*: "When I tell you that I am interested in silence, what do you think of? What can you tell me?"
> *Professor*: "Well, one thing I will begin with: When you are talking, I am not really silent. Silence is 'I am listening to you.' It seems to me that out of silence comes the word. At

---

[1]DeMuth, Philip. "Eliza and Her Offspring" in *Literature and Medicine,* Vol. 4: *Psychiatry and Medicine,* edited by Peter W. Graham. Baltimore: Johns Hopkins University Press, 1985, pp. 138-39.
[2]*Ibid.*

first, there is silence, and then there is the word, so that
without silence there can be no creativity. I think the
problem is expressed by the Buddhists – that the mind is a
kind of monkey, and it's hard to tame it. It's jumping
around all over the place. I can experience silence, but it's
almost like I have to be distracted to do that. So, one way
I have been able to do that is through drumming, and
having something, in a sense, distracting my mind process."

Harry: "Would you talk about drumming? It is noise. It is
rhythm. It is music. It is sound. How does that create
silence for you?"

Professor: "Well, yeah, it's an outer distraction-noise that
[pause] silence has to be in it. I mean [pause] silence would
have to be the silence within, so that it is beating out other
noises. These noises stay, but it's beating the noise inside,
or fooling the mind in a way, – tricking it to stop. [Pause]
Silence to me also seems to be timeless. When one is in
silence, one is not aware of the ticking of the clock inside
oneself. Out of that comes my creativity."

Harry: "When you think of silent places, what occurs to
you?"

Professor: "Well, first of all darkness, kind of like Genesis."

Harry: "The Darkness."

Professor: "Yes. The spirit hovering above the Darkness.
Peace. Tranquillity. I think of the north – the direction of
the North – and I think of snow and the white. You know,
like in a snowstorm: you are blinded. And it seems like in
a Silence, you have to be blinded or deafened, in a way. The
Arctic silence. Other than that, just images come."

Harry: "Well, we have a paradox in carrying on a conversation about silence, don't we?"

Professor: "Exactly! [laughter] We don't let the silence
continue very long."

Harry: "I am reminded of the Tao: 'He who talks does not
know. And he who knows does not talk.'"

Professor: "Exactly. And the same with the *Upanishads* or
Hinduism."

Harry: "For example?"

Professor: "Well, exactly what you are saying: He who knows about being Brahman cannot speak of it, and he who speaks of it, does not know it. So, Brahman is silent, and you can't use words to describe it. Of course, the Upanishad is all words, but that is what we are talking about."

Harry: "Words."

The professor then speaks of the mythology of Trickster Monkey. Darkness and North are not associated with creativity but with cold, sterility, Satan, freezing, and death. North is the direction of the end of the earth. He emphasizes the world of the spirit and the visions of Eastern philosophy and religion in contrast to the Western culture of words, science, and reason.

Shaw's play, based on the mythology of Pygmalion, was adapted in the musical, *My Fair Lady*, in which Professor Henry Higgins achieves scientific triumph in transforming Eliza from a street urchin flower girl into an elegant, lovely, articulate woman. When Eliza returns from a triumphant performance at the grand ball where she was accepted as a Hungarian princess of royal blood, Professor Higgins spouts endless words of self-congratulation and ignores Eliza, who sings of the folly of words in place of love:

> Words
> Words
> Words.
> I am sick of words.
> I get them all day through.
> First from him
> Now from you.
> Is that all you blighters can do?
> Show me!
> SHOW ME![1]

[1]Lerner, Alan Jay. *My Fair Lady* (adaptation and lyrics). New York: Coward-McCann, 1956. (Music by Frederick Lowe.)

It is important that both man and woman can balance silent and talk space, like quanta listening.

My wife and I have solved this problem of who speaks and who listens silently, who is right and who is wrong, by adopting this pragmatic and firm rule: We agree that on Mondays, Wednesdays, and Fridays Jane knows everything, and that on Tuesdays, Thursdays, and Saturdays I know everything. That leaves Sunday when nobody knows anything. It works because if we get into a fight one of us will invoke the fool-proof equation that never fails to amuse us.

Naturally it helps to have a sense of humor. When someone at a cocktail party told Dorothy Parker that she was outspoken, Dorothy replied, "By whom?" The telephone can outtalk me when I am put on hold and flooded with inane messages I do not want to hear, music to send a message, and various comments that public relations people have programmed to regurgitate on the hapless person on hold.

The American addiction to gap-talking in order to obliterate silent spaces is magnified on radio. There is a continuous seepage of word noise on talk shows like toxic pollutants of the airways. Radio is a model of serious gap-filling noise. It is so ubiquitous that it profoundly influences the American psyche. We become radios.

Max Picard says that the world of radio is based on the noise of words:

> Radio is a machine producing absolute verbal noise. The content hardly matters any longer; the production of noise is the main concern. It is as though words were being ground down by radio, transformed into an amorphous mass.
>
> There is no silence in radio or true words either, for a situation has been created in which silence is no longer missed and words are no longer missed either, in which words are ground down to mere radio-noise, in which everything is present and at the same time nothing is present. ...

Everything on radio is constantly on the move, in a state of perpetual flux; nothing is concretely fixed and stable. Past, present and future are all mixed up together in one long drawn-out noise. ...

Wireless sets are like constantly firing automatic pistols shooting at silence.

Behind all this noise the enemy lurks in hiding: silence.

The noise of radio is becoming more and more violent, because the fear is becoming more and more acute that it may suddenly be attacked by silence and the real world.[1]

I have written a radio script entitled:

Always It Is Silent or It Is Not Silent:
A Tautology in Three Acts

ACT ONE: The Silent Scream Is the Curse of Silence
Man: Yes (applause)
Woman: Yes (louder applause)
Chorus: Yes (silence)

ACT TWO: Just Say No and Say No More
Man: No (applause)
Woman: No (no applause)
Chorus: No (torpor)

ACT THREE: Silence Is a Blessing and a Damnation
Man: Yes (drum roll)
Woman: No (church bells)
Chorus: Yes (stupor)

---

[1]Picard, *World of Silence*, pp. 189-90, 209.

On Doing Nothing

I telephoned my Jungian analyst in San Francisco, Joseph Henderson, to congratulate him on his ninety-second birthday (September 10, 1995). He was vigorous, alert, still practicing, and highly articulate. The following is a transcription of part of our conversation:

Joe: "Rollo May's wife gave a birthday party for me and Helena [Joe's wife] last night, and I was saying that I had been to my ophthalmologist this spring. He is a new man, and he and his assistant were very interested in me because I am still working at my age. So they were asking me questions about it. I told them that I take one week a month off from seeing patients. My ophthalmologist said, 'What do you do with your week off?' And I said, 'Nothing.' That absolutely fascinated them as they thought it spoke to the kind of workaholic attitude of modern professional life. One of them told me recently, 'You know, I took off the month of July and did nothing!' In other words, that concept of nothing balances too much activity."

Harry: "That's the basis of my book."

Joe: "Sure. It must be."

Harry: "Sometimes after a busy day, I just sit in my study and do nothing. I may hold my cat on my lap for an hour and just sit still. Sometimes I doze. Mitten is the quietest, most alert animal to sounds – turns and cups his ears like radar antennae tracking sounds I cannot hear. I used to think that sitting and doing nothing was wasting time."

Joe: "That helps the psyche catch up with itself, and you get a new life, a new spirit."

Let Us Not Forget Pooh Bear

... said Christopher Robin, "but what I like doing best is
Nothing."
"How do you do Nothing?" asked Pooh, after he had
wondered for a long time.
"Well, it's when people call out at you just as you're going
off to do it, 'What are you going to do, Christopher Robin?'
and you say, 'Oh, nothing,' and you go and do it."
"Oh, I see," said Pooh.
"This is a nothing sort of thing that we're doing now."
"Oh, I see," said Pooh again.
"It means just going along, listening to all the things you
can't hear, and not bothering."
"Oh!" said Pooh.[1]

A Zenrin poem says:

Sitting quietly, doing nothing,
Spring comes, and the grass grows by itself.[2]

In Jewish life, Shabbat, the sabbath, was the time to stop
doing in the ordinary world and to study the Torah, sing,
dance, celebrate, and reflect on the previous six days. Arthur
Washkow, director of the Salam Center, said in an article on
the early Jewish monks, who were called Therapeutae:

If there were a single piece of Jewish wisdom that was the
most important to impart to the human race at this very
moment in history it would be the importance of the
Shabbat. I mean the generally profound sense of pausing
to be, to reflect, and to break the addiction to working,
producing, making, inventing. We need to be able to say,
"Hey! We have done extraordinary things, now let us
pause."[3]

---

[1]Milne, A. A. *The House at Pooh Corner*. New York: Dutton, 1928, pp. 172-73.
[2]Zenrin in *The Way of Zen* by Alan W. Watts. New York: New American
Library/Mentor Book, 1957, p. 133.
[3]Washkow, Arthur (from an interview with Martin Marty), in *Context*, April
1996, p. 6.

When Americans want silence, they usually want other people to be silent so they can speak for and of themselves. A cartoon in the *New Yorker* showed a tall man talking down to a woman at a cocktail party, saying, "Let's go somewhere I can talk." Silence, listening, pausing, and doing nothing compulsively require discipline and techniques so we can make ourselves not be doing and not be talking. In the American culture of individuality and free speech, there is a premium on speaking up, saying what's on your mind – in short, getting it out. Individuality becomes individualism, with all the darkness of "isms." Couple this notion with the American expectation to be first, biggest, best, and always a winner and you have explosive noises and violence.

When I am caught in me-me-me-me conversations, with overlapping dialogues reaching intolerable noise, I become quiet and withdrawn or turn on my selective inattention and cool indifference rather than dial 911 or 1-800-SHUTUP.

Many years ago, when I was treating a patient whom I found boring or too demanding, or sitting in dull lectures where I felt compelled to stay, I squelched the urge to say something extremely critical or boldly state my truth. Then I discovered that I was doodling an "S" that overlapped a "U." It looked like this:

After a while, I realized that the letters "S" and "U" stood for Stanford University. One day while supervising a Stanford psychiatric resident who was reporting a case he was treating, I could see that he believed that what he said was brilliant and ingenious. I thought he was insensitive, and for a highly intelligent doctor, being stupid like only a person with a very high IQ is capable of. I muted my critical comments until I realized he had begun to play the role of teacher-supervisor to me. At this point, I noticed that my doodle had grown a new curlicue, like a tail on the "U." It looked like this:

The addition appeared as the letter "P" and the doodle was no longer "S-U" but "S-U-P," a shorthand sign to myself that I read as "SHUT UP!"

Only retreat into attentive silence would allow my anger to cool. Then maybe I could lead the resident into critical self-scrutiny. I was not very optimistic. I needed to take time off and do nothing while giving up the attempt to change him.

I have since used this moniker when I become aware that someone is strongly objecting to my opinion and does not even want to hear it. This usually means transference if my opinions are taken as a personal affront. I doodle my self-imposed silence and wait.

Just as it is important to learn silence and listening, it is equally important to know when and how to speak out. On this score, I cite Socrates's maxim: *primum non tacere*, meaning: "First no silence; that is, speak up!" Learning to speak up spontaneously, honestly, and for oneself is a task that almost all of the people who consult me need to learn.

When people are afraid to speak out, intimidated by outer or inner forces, they brood, feel depressed, and commonly assume passive or active meanness to ward off their fears. Once they face the snarling, blaming bully within, their hostile and envious thoughts diminish.

Our propensity to speak up and speak out is determined by our natural temperament, typology, genetic propensities, and environment. People from New York and very large cities are usually more outspoken and argumentative than people from typical rural places. As a general rule, the extravert is compelled to talk and relate and even welcome interactive conflict, in contrast to the introvert, who withdraws, holds back, restrains talking, and avoids confrontations. Extraverted American gap fillers are acquisitive, filling up space with material objects and enjoying the envy of others – witness TV advertisements for new cars.

Thomas Merton, who became a monk at the Trappist monastery of Our Lady of Gethsemane in Kentucky, described his first night at the monastery:

The embrace of it, the silence! I had entered into a solitude that was an impregnable fortress. And the silence that enfolded me, spoke to me, and spoke louder and more eloquently than any voice and in the middle of that quiet, clean-smelling room, with the moon pouring in through the open window, with the warm night air, I realized truly whose house that was, O glorious Mother of God. ... Notre Dame, Notre Dame, all around the world, Notre Dame de Gethsemani.[1]

Prophesy at the Threshold

Beside the back door of my greenhouse, I have hung an aluminum medallion which reads: "Bidden or Not Bidden, God Is Present." These words are the translation of the Latin words carved in stone over the front door to C. G. Jung's home in Küsnacht, Switzerland: VOCATUS ATQUE NON VOCATUS DEUS ADERIT.

This saying is often noted by admirers of Jung to state, in a sentimental way, that the loving spirit of God will be present whether one wishes it or not. These words are Erasmus' Latin translation of the Greek words of warning that the Delphi Oracle gave the Lacedaemonians when they were planning war against Athens. Jung explained:

> It says, yes, the god will be on the spot, but in what form and to what purpose? I have put the inscription there to remind my patients and myself: Timor dei initium sapientae [Psalm 111:10]. The fear of the Lord is the beginning of wisdom. Here another not less important road begins, not the approach to "Christianity" but to God himself and this seems to be the ultimate question.[2]

[1]Merton, Thomas. *The Seven Storey Mountain*. New York: Signet Book/New American Library, 1962, pp. 314-15.
[2]Jung, C. G. *Word and Image* edited by Aniela Jaffé. Princeton, N.J.: Princeton University Press, 1979, pp. 136-39.

I have often walked through that door but it never occurred to me that the words carved above were a warning: to fear whatever form God assumed when I was planning to attack an enemy. I had always felt a glow, that it meant I was entering a sacred place.

Most Jungian students and analysts who know that these words stand over the majestic front door of Jung's home assume a purely religious viewpoint, that the Wise Old Man was reminding those who walked through his front door that God would be present – engraved in stone – and don't forget it. Many admirers of Jung are in awe of this pronouncement. Since they are the words of the Delphi Oracle, awe is not inappropriate.

Being a Jungian analyst, I find the concept of the archetype of theoretical and practical significance. The archetype is a potential form that is realized in countless symbols and embodiments and in instinctual patterns of behavior. Jung conceived the archetypes of a priori patterns for universal symbols, like father or mother. Father becomes the father, who becomes a specific father. Silence per se has no purpose or expression. When it is actualized as a sound in speech, it is called by the name silence. Silence is not an archetype; it is unnamable, and unknowable. When it is expressed in a word, it is no longer silent. I will try to convey these thoughts in whimsical poems on mind and body:

MIND

> Silence has no nitty gritty
> To get down to.
> Silence has no point.
> So I cannot give you the point I am making.
> I can make noise.
> I cannot make silence.
> Silence has no direction.
> It is everywhere;
> Up/down; in/out; N.S.E. & W.

You cannot locate silence on a map
Or with a computer.
Silence has no nitty.
Silence has no gritty.
For the intellectual,
That is a pity.

BODY

We have no earlids.
Eyelids, yes.
No earlids.
We have no body curtains to close off sound.

We have a pair of ears, a pair of eyes
And a paradox of silence.
We do not see all the time
Because we blink.
All the time, we are hearing something
From every direction all around us.
We do not have to turn our heads to hear
Like we do to see.

We are always listening in some fashion.
All we can hear is within the sound range
Of 20 to 20,000 vibrations per second.
My cat can do better.
Schizophrenic patients hear voices
I cannot hear.

Hannah Merker lost almost total hearing at the age of thirty-nine when, skiing for the first time in her life, she fell and had a concussion: "When I opened my eyes, I was on my back. I could see that people were talking, a movie with the sound system suddenly silenced." Her plight was different from the congenitally deaf, who exist in silence never having heard or listened. Realizing that "silence makes us listeners," Merker wrote an autobiography twenty-two years after her accident. She learned American Sign Language, but her remarkable "hearing-ear" dog, Sheena, became her constant guide and protector. Merker's affectionate dog was invaluable in noisy New York City where she lives. Like the Seeing Eye dog, the animal-human bonding reflects a primitive deep connection between the human and the animal world.[1]

Threat of Death

When I reflect on seriously difficult times in my life and realize how these adversities and tragic events have, in the end, given me new life, I recall Hugh Downs' interview with a blind man: "Have you been blind all your life?" The man replied, "Not yet."

After graduating from the University of Minnesota Medical School in 1940, I went to the Panama Canal Zone to intern at the Gorgas Memorial Hospital. Gorgas was an army hospital and I held a reserve commission in the navy. I was convinced that the United States was about to be involved in World War II and was eager to finish the internship so I could go on active duty in the navy, aboard a cruiser in the Pacific.

I was twenty-four years old and in excellent health when I began my internship. While I was on the infectious disease service, I remember a Dutch sailor dying with miliary (widely disseminated) tuberculosis, vomiting bloody sputum on me.

It was the rainy season, and daily tropical downpours drenched Panama. Soon I began to have insomnia with night sweats, steady loss of weight, and a productive cough. It did not occur to me that I was developing tuberculosis. I was pleased to look in trim shape, and had my picture taken in my white navy uniform to send home to my girlfriend and parents. From our screened-in intern quarters, we could see the Panama Canal and the large naval vessels going by. From nearby airfields, we could hear the fighter planes preparing to

[1]Merker, Hannah. *Listening: Ways of Hearing in a Silent World*. New York: Harper-Collins, 1994.

defend Panama. A national emergency had been declared for the military services.

I bought a case of Ballantine Scotch at the PX, put it under my bed, and drank myself to sleep every night while working twelve-hour days on the surgical service. One morning I was aware that I had a high fever, and went to see my doctor – examination, chest x-ray, sputum tests. He told me that I had extensive tuberculosis of the left upper lobe of my lung. Holding up my x-rays, the doctor pointed to a large cavity in the apex where the disease was already moderately far advanced. He told me that since I had tuberculosis, they would have to evacuate me to the States. Then he made a curious statement that confused me: "You are a doctor and know about tuberculosis, so I won't have to tell you about it." When he left, questions distressed me, but when the word *tuberculosis* was spoken, everything I had ever known about it evaporated from my mind. I was not there.

It is important for the reader to realize that in 1940, tuberculosis was still called "The Captain of Death" and "The White Plague." It killed many young doctors. Another classmate of mine developed tuberculosis during his internship and died. At this time, there were no medications to treat tuberculosis. None at all. The cure was total bed rest, for months, or years. You lived in isolation in sanatoria hidden in the country, like being exiled on an island whose inhabitants bear a dark stigma. Doctors, nurses, aides, and the very few friends who are brave enough to visit wear masks and white coats to protect themselves from you. Patients were first confined to bed twenty-four hours a day. Regular sputum examinations are made until the tubercle bacilli disappear. At this point, when patients are no longer contagious, they can move around in a wheelchair, and occasionally leave the hospital if someone will take them for a drive. It is a great struggle in acculturation to a dangerous foreign place.[1]

[1]Wilmer, Harry A. "A Hitherto Undescribed Island: An Approach to the Problem of Acculturation," *American Scientist*, Vol. 41, No. 3, July 1953.

In Panama, while on the ear, nose, and throat service at Gorgas Hospital, the doctors went to see the patients at the Coca Sola Leprosarium. There I saw the deformed, forgotten lepers – with mutilated hands and feet, white anesthetic lesions in the skin, and ear, nose, and throat lesions – sitting on screened-in porches staring forlornly at visitors to the leper colony.

The leper bacillus looks like the tubercle bacillus. There was no effective medical treatment for either one. I would know the solitude of isolation and slow-time, not calculated in the hours of the day, but in slow-time calculated by the months, and ticking off the years on the calendar. Outside the window of my room, the top of a poplar tree brushed by, whose leaves I saw fall twice.

I was far from the noise of the coming war, the sounds of combat, inside large cruisers, and cannons firing. That would be like a dream from which I was trying to wake up to join in the real world. For months, the only live connections with the sounds of the other world I heard came through the radio headset with earphones plugged into a socket in the wall behind my bed. The radio was a blessing, up to a point – until the terrible sounds I heard when I awoke from the mandatory noon-hour nap and plugged in at one o'clock on December 7, 1941. The first reports were coming in from Pearl Harbor announcing the Japanese attack. Like Americans everywhere, I was stunned. My closest friend was on the battleship USS *California*, and the next day I read in the paper that he was the first war dead from Minnesota.

My white naval officer uniform with the black and gold shoulder boards, along with my cap with the beautiful gold navy insignia, were stored in the basement of the sanatorium. They would begin to rot before I would ever be able to put them on during the Korean War, when I was finally able to get back into the navy. You see, active duty had been a childhood ambition ever since my father had taken me onto a heavy navy cruiser in the port of New Orleans in 1920. I still have the photograph of me standing beneath the huge guns of a turret next to two handsome marines in dress uniform. Man, that was living – or so it seemed to me.

I flew from Panama back to the University of Minnesota Hospital, stopping on the way to see my father for the last time. He was dying of metastatic cancer in the Touro Infirmary in New Orleans. He had gone back home from Minnesota to die, and I was going back home to Minnesota – maybe to die. Dad must not know, I thought.

In New Orleans, I went to my mother's apartment near the hospital, sat in the bed, and told her that I had tuberculosis and was going to Minnesota to go into the hospital. Mother was exhausted and depressed from visiting my father every day in the hospital. I appeared with no warning to tell her that I was seriously ill. Never before or since have I dreaded breaking bad news of illness as much as that afternoon.

I said that I was not going to tell Dad the truth. Then I dressed up in my starched white Navy uniform, put on my cap at a slight angle, and marched with mother into father's room. He was emaciated, in great pain, and did not have long to live. After greetings and inquiries about his health, and without the slightest twinge of guilt, I told him that I had orders to sea aboard a heavy cruiser and was on my way to the coast to meet my ship. Dad brightened, smiled broadly – and sadly – obviously proud and reassured. Many times before, Dad told me that in case of war, he wanted me to be a medical officer mending people, and not killing them. It was a sentimental moment when we embraced and told each other farewell.

I went back to my mother's apartment, packed my uniform, and headed for the airport. I had nausea, great weakness, and felt faint as we airport-hopped in our DC3 all the way home.

At the university hospital, my family doctor met and examined me. The next day, he told me that he would have to send me to the county sanitorium at Glen Lake that afternoon. I was driven in a luxurious new Cadillac ambulance. Arriving in style, I was wheeled on a gurney into the admitting office, welcomed, and handed a piece of paper to sign. On the paper was printed "Pauper's Oath." It was necessary to sign it to be admitted to the county hospital. I had no option. I had dropped out of the sky and had nowhere else to go.

Then I was hit by the "Why me?" syndrome. Why tuberculosis? Why a dying father? Why this humiliation and shame dumped on me – this helpless dependent young doctor, cut down in the prime of his life? Only in later life did I learn the profound answer to this common life-crisis question – namely, "Why not me? Who am I to be so special that I could not be wounded by the slings and arrows of human life? Why not me, so that I might learn of my own mortality and the need for inspiration, and the healing of the soul?"

I was wheeled to a room where there were two other young patients: one, a doctor, the other a newspaper reporter. They seemed good enough and had not been expecting me – although the one empty bed in the room was a gap that would inevitably be filled, until the time came when there were specific antibiotics. In a little while, two gaunt, somber men wearing white jackets came to my bedside. One stood at the foot of the bed, the other at the head. They took out a tape measure and without a word measured me from head to foot. One of them shook his head and mumbled, "We are measuring you for a coffin." Dead silence. The other said, "Is that you coffin?" I made myself laugh along with the other four. So much for the initiation ritual.

My roommate, Feike Feikema, a six-foot four-inch giant of a newspaper reporter, was writing a novel in bed. The other roommate was a laborer who drank beer when his friends sneaked it into the room. The novel that Feike wrote entitled *Boy Almighty*, was the story of the three of us in that sanatorium room. (I die on the operating table.)

Feike Feikema, of Frisian ancestry, later changed his name to Manfred Feikema and pursued a successful lifelong career as a novelist after his discharge from the hospital. In his commentary on our special relationship, his intuition revealed a sensitive insight into my inner being and a prophetic portrayal of my life for the next decade – except for my untimely death as Dr. Theodore Fawkes in his novel.[1]

As Feike quipped, I caught the writing bug from him and began to fantasize about a cartoon educational book on tuberculosis. One morning, as Feike and I were bantering about the story I wanted to write, the name *Huber the Tuber* flashed into my mind. Instantly I knew I would write a book called *Huber the Tuber: The Lives and Loves of a Tubercle Bacillus*. With my fountain pen, I began drawing pictures of Huber in a large drawing book.

This activity was disparaged by the nurses. I went undercover, drawing under the covers and hiding the manuscript. For 163 days, I drew one illustration a day, and wrote one paragraph narrative, and one brief scientific explanation of the story of tuberculosis as revealed by the adventures of Huber in my lungs. It was a serious, but light-hearted book because I wanted to reach a frightened audience, especially children, to help break the stigma associated with TB. I thought that when I left the sanatorium I did not want to face the outside world feeling ashamed. It seemed better to have produced a whimsical story of successful outcome of an ordeal. In the end, Huber falls asleep trapped in an air cell of the lung, in the cavity that had been dug by Göbbels and Göring. The tuberculosis was arrested.

My experience of eleven months in the sanatorium would always help me understand the illness from the perspective of the patient. I would forever remember that when I was depressed and told my doctor, he did not understand or really listen. He prescribed phenobarbital that made me drowsy. One day, however, the hospital social worker came and sat by my bed and asked me to talk to her about my feelings. I think that my doctor might have sent her. She was the first person to sit down and listen in silence without moralizing or giving me good advice that was no good. She listened. She was silent. I felt I was understood. I was less at war with myself – less sorry for myself and more at peace.

[1]Feikema, Feike. *Boy Almighty*. St. Paul, Minn.: Itasca Press, 1945, pp. 265-75.

Long hospital confinement with tuberculosis had an effect on me, as it has on many gifted people. One is cut off from life for a long inner journey – somewhat like a sojourn in a monastery for introspection – and reflection on life and death. Such an experience can be a stimulus for creative powers to expression, according to the particular talents of the sufferer. It gave me a spiritual opportunity to transcend the mundane and hope for repair of body and psyche, a type of wholeness. These are the reflections of an old man, not the way I saw the experience at the time when I lost the love of my life, and my father, and was more estranged from my mother who, having just lost her husband, seemed to have no comprehension for my most important feelings.

I spent the last months of my hospital cure at Trudeau Sanatorium, Saranac Lake, New York, in the beautiful Adirondack Mountains. There I made the final forty India ink sketches and edited the text of *Huber*. The manuscript was rejected by twelve major presses largely because of the doubts and fears that a humorous cartoon book about tuberculosis would not sell. Since I knew the pathology, treatment, and symptoms of the disease, there were never any questions about the authenticity of the book. At last, Lippincott was willing to publish the book provided the National Tuberculosis Association (now the American Lung Association) would endorse it. I brought the publisher's letter and manuscript to the medical director of the association, Dr. Henry Kleinschmidt. He was immediately enthusiastic and easily persuaded me to let the National Tuberculosis Association be the publisher. They would boost its sales along with the Christmas Seals, and their national school educational programs.

To my surprise, the book sold almost seventy thousand hardcover copies and received all excellent reviews. Many readers wrote me. The most memorable letter was from a girl in elementary school scolding me because after Huber fell in love with Bovy – a bovine TB bacillus he met in the Old Knee Joint – they settled down in a lung cell where Bovy fell into the Old Blood Stream and was never heard from again! The girl insisted that I tell her what happened to Bovy. I wrote and explained that Bovy was finally washed up on the shore of the Old Blood Stream and ultimately (after this book story) found Huber. I drew a picture of Bovy explaining her own predicament and sent it to the little girl, who then wrote me that she was very happy.

It should come as no surprise that this book was written by a sick sailor during the grim first year of World War II as a war story of the Great Battlefield in Lungland, where Nasty non Sputum, Rusty the Bloodyvitch, and their cohorts were conquered. I drew a map of the war as endplates inside the covers at the beginning and end of the book.[1]

[1]Wilmer, Harry A. *Huber the Tuber: The Lives and Loves of a Tubercle Bacillus.* New York: National Tuberculosis Association, 1st ed., 1942.

5

War

But, in a larger sense, we cannot dedicate – we cannot consecrate – we cannot hallow – this ground. The brave men, living and dead, who struggled here, have consecrated it, far above our poor power to add or detract. The world will little note, nor long remember, what we say here, but it can never forget what they did here.

– Abraham Lincoln
The Gettysburg Address, 1863

We have remembered what Lincoln said there, although the people present did not hear him, but we have forgotten the brave men, living and dead, who struggled there. We perpetually forget, rather than remember, the sacrifices people made in wars for causes they did not understand. The Vietnam Memorial in Washington, D.C., is an exception, a created symbol of reverence, silence, and grief. Americans have forgotten the sacrifices of our soldiers in Korea. We ignore or keep forgetting the carnage committed in the name of power, exploitation, race, religion, and nation. The ideals of God, family, and country still exist but are increasingly tarnished and betrayed. And yet, hope lies in the mysteries of God, family, and country – spirit – relationship – love – place.

Shooting wars are as great a noise as we can manufacture. In the midst of combat, soldiers and sailors must endure fire, smoke, screams, and cries on the battlefield. They have no alternative to listening to the terrifying screech of bullets, shells, napalm, grenades, rockets, and bombs. They cannot escape seeing their buddies killed or maimed, or experiencing angry and eager slaughter. At home, they must endure their grief alone because few people have the stomach to listen to the stories and emotions of survivors. In general, veterans sense that it is almost impossible to break through the collective amnesia that we all have for the primal horror of war – for hell, pandemonium, and purgatory.

Some gifted people write, paint, photograph, and compose poetry or music about the universal feelings of war. It is safe to say that almost no one who has not been under close and continuous fire on the battlefield has the slightest idea of what combat veterans experienced and the guilt they have.

Those who remain at home are deaf and blind. They do not long remember, because they naturally prefer to forget so they can accumulate material possessions, nurture greed, and pursue the illusion of security without awareness of guilt. I suspect that we are all unconsciously afraid that once the monster of war would be recognized and let out, it would be *Apocalypse Now*.

We are more or less helpless during catastrophes, accidents, horrors of Nature, abuse, and cruel and terrible acts of mindless behavior being committed. Afterward, trying to get comfort from reason, we conjure up opinions of whys and hows it could have happened. We pay attention to the statistics of public opinion polls, to media experts and answer-givers who come out of knotholes, worm holes, or brainy and political institutions to point fingers of blame. I remind you of the words of Eric Hoffer, longshoreman philosopher: "One of the surprising privileges of intellectuals is that they are free to be scandalously asinine without harming their reputations."[1] Small comfort. Solace if it is to come will not be from reason but wisdom.

Today we store the packages of ultimate noise in our hordes of atomic and hydrogen bombs, in underworld silos

[1]Hoffer, Eric. *Before the Sabbath*. New York: Harper & Row, 1979, p. 3.

and large stockpiles in poorly guarded ammunition warehouses.

The history of civilized nations and the atomic bomb is most discouraging. The Big Bang that marked creation of the universe is ready to happen again to end it. The deed, not the sound, will mark the end of civilization. The atomic bomb is the shadow of the slowly eroding civility in civilization.

We have forgotten the history and unconscionable cruelty of wars and power-mad dictators. In the face of torture, we turn not the other cheek but the head. The airways are deluged with noise. Where is the silence in which we can listen and think about what we are doing to ourselves and our children?

We declare war on poverty and crime. We make a lot of noise about those wars and accomplish little. We declare ourselves for human rights, freedom, and the pursuit of happiness but we commit deeds that intensify poverty, dividing the nation between "haves" and "have nots." The problem is that we are silent when we should speak out and speak out when we should be silent.

Let us explore war in the context of noise and silence.

A Noiseless Blast

Hiroshima
8:15 a.m., August 6, 1945

There was no sound of planes. The morning was still; the place was cool and pleasant. Then a tremendous flash of light cut across the sky from east to west, from the city toward the hills. It seemed a sheet of sun. … Almost no one in Hiroshima recalls hearing any noise of the bomb. But a fisherman in his sampan on the Inland Sea near Tsuzu … saw the flash and heard a tremendous explosion; he was nearly twenty miles from Hiroshima, but the thunder was greater than when the B-29s hit Iwakuni, only five miles away. ... Under what seemed to be a local dust cloud, the day grew darker and darker.[1]

Nagasaki
11:02 a.m., August 9, 1945

It was just after 11 a.m. I heard a low droning sound, like that of distant aeroplane engines. ... At the same time the sound of the plane's engines, growing louder and louder, seemed to swoop down over the hospital. ... There was a blinding white flash of light, and the next moment – Bang! Crack! A huge impact like a gigantic blow smote down upon our bodies, our heads, our hospital. I lay flat – I didn't know whether or not of my own volition. Then came piles of debris, slamming into my back ... looking to the south-west, I was stunned. The sky was as dark as pitch, covered with dense clouds of smoke; under that blackness, over the earth, hung a yellow-brown fog. Gradually the veiled ground became visible, and the view beyond rooted me to the spot with horror. All the buildings I could see were on fire. ... In the afternoon a change was noticeable in the appearance of the injured who came up to the hospital. The crowd of ghosts which looked whitish in the morning were now turned black. Their hair was burnt; their skin was charred and blackened, blistered and peeled. ... "Are you a doctor? Please, if you wouldn't mind, could you examine me?" So said a young man.

In the Atlantic, President Truman was speeding back to America on board the cruiser Augusta. When he heard the news he exclaimed, "This is the greatest thing in history!"[2]

[1]Hersey, John. *Hiroshima*. New York: Bantam, 1979, pp. 6-7.
[2]Azizuki, Tatsuichiro. *Nagasaki 1945*. London: Quartet Books, 1981, pp. 14, 111, 25-27, 32.

The Sky Gaps

Large holes in the ozone layer of the earth's atmosphere were discovered in the sky by scientists from the Arctic island of Spitsbergen. An ozone hole is an ominous gap that we cannot fill. The ozone acts as a barrier against ultraviolet radiation from the sun. We have created the gap through the widespread use of chlorfluorocarbons that are used in many industrial processes and aerosol propellants. It is a hole through which the sun can invade civilization and the human body, causing skin cancers and cataracts. In a medieval metaphor, it is as if The Walled City of Earth has been breached.

The Mountain Gaps

America spread west through the Cumberland Gap, a natural passage through the Cumberland Mountains formed by erosion from a stream. The gap was discovered in 1750 by a land exploration company, and was Daniel Boone's wilderness road to blaze a trail to Kentucky. The Cumberland Gap was held alternately by the Confederate and Union forces during the American Civil War. The gap was too useful and too vast to be plugged.

When President Jefferson sent the Lewis and Clark Expedition to claim the West, there were no roads beyond the mountains, only trails. There were no power sources other than people's muscles, falling water, and wind. The most dangerous factor was the Indians, whose territory the explorers were invading. The Lewis and Clark Expedition was small, so as not to alarm the Indians, whom they placated with talk, beads, trinkets, whiskey, gunpowder, and firearms. They gave the chiefs medallions of President Jefferson, who, they promised, was now their benevolent Great Father protector. Lewis and Clark used every trick possible to get the land away from the Indians – the lurking enemy. Americans rushed through gaps and mountain passes, and sailed the rivers scouting a war between Americans and Indians. Cruelty and barbarism characterized both sides.

Stephen Ambrose wrote the story of the Lewis and Clark Expedition and Thomas Jefferson. He said:

> Hypocrisy ran through the Indian policy, as it did through the policies of his predecessors and successors. Join us or get out of the way, the Americans said to the Indians, but in fact the Indians could do neither. ... In fact he [Jefferson] stole all the land he could from Indians east of the Mississippi while preparing those west of the river for the same fate, after the beaver were trapped out.
> How could the greatest champion of human rights in American history do such a thing?. ... Anyway, no matter how much compassion Jefferson felt toward the Indians, however badly he wanted law and order and bureaucratic regularity on the frontier, on this question the people, not the government, ruled. Americans had but one Indian policy – get out or get killed – and it was non-negotiable.[1]

Our history of expansion to the West began by embarking on a premeditated war. In another century, gap-filling Americans rushed from east to west, hell-bent to reach the West in the Gold Rush. Once again, the idea that Nature abhors a vacuum can be applied. Americans saw the West as empty, a land of Terra Nullus – freestanding wilderness to be claimed.

Max Picard said that the man who has become lost in the noise is saved by the firm structure of war, even by the firm structure of brutal action. "That is why it is so easy to make war and commit brutalities in the world of noise. War and bombs are absorbed by the vacuum of this world of noise."[2]

American genocide? Slavery? Twentieth-century civilization had returned to genocide in Europe, Russia, Africa, the

[1]Ambrose, Stephen. *Undaunted Courage: Meriwether Lewis, Thomas Jefferson, and the Opening of the American West.* New York: Touchstone Books, 1996, p. 548.
[2]Picard, Max. *World of Silence*, p. 18.

Near East, and the Far East. In reading the history of war, it seems that the human psyche has a recurrent tendency to run amok. What civilized people avoid recognizing is that they are all capable of brutality, murder, and violence. These capabilities may be under good control, but they still exist in the human psyche. These dark forces are not necessarily explainable in terms of childhood development, but rather as characteristics of the collective unconscious of all people. This was Jung's idea of that part of the human condition that is unrelated to our personal lives, and being unconscious – by its nature – we are not conscious of it. We are apt to see it in other people or project it onto them. It is one of the fears that invites war and noise.

The Spanish philosopher, José Ortega y Gasset, reminds us that when we have nothing to say about a matter, instead of keeping quiet, we do the opposite: we shout. "And the shout is the sonorous preliminary to aggression, to combat, to slaughter."[1]

Northrup Frye, a Canadian literary critic, told this fascinating story: The typical random victim of a tragedy is innocent in the sense that what happens to him is far greater than what anything he has done provokes, like the mountaineer whose shout brings down an avalanche. He is guilty in the sense that he is a member of a guilty society, or living in a world where such injustices are an inescapable part of existence.[2]

Twice I have been stunned and terrified in the Swiss Alps by sudden explosive thunder, only to realize that it was the cannonade sound of an avalanche, close enough that it might be headed for me.

[1]Ortega y Gasset, José. *Man and People*. New York: W. W. Norton, 1957, p. 15.
[2]Frye, Northrup. *Anatomy of Criticism: Four Essays*. Princeton, N.J.: Princeton University Press, 1973, p. 41.

Synchronicity?

This morning when I took my walk, Mitten kept a few paces ahead of me. It was raining slightly. The sky was unpleasantly dark. I did not hear the birds, but I did hear the roar of the highway. Then it seemed momentarily quiet, a calm before a storm. We walked on. Mitten was unperturbed. Lightning crashed.

I thought I should go into the house and get away from the trees. Distant thunder rumbled but it was interrupted by a short burst of thunder without lightning. I knew that this was the sound of cannons firing at nearby Fort Hood where the Third Corps, First Cavalry, was on maneuvers. A helicopter whirled loud and low overhead. The rain began to fall in great sheets of water while a lightning bolt struck somewhere near. Mitten and I ran to my greenhouse. I sat at my desk with Mitten curled up at my feet. A book was lying in front of me on my desk: Dalton Trumbo's *Johnny Got His Gun*.

I had no recollection of putting it on my desk. Did Jane put it there? She hardly ever comes into the greenhouse. Maybe I had put it there and forgotten it. I had no memory of how it happened to be there.

This antiwar book was first published in 1939 just as World War II began. It is about a soldier, age twenty, whose face was blown off in World War I. He was not only totally blind and deaf but he had also lost both arms and legs. He was a torso with brains, unable to move, confined in a hospital room by himself in total darkness and silence, unable to smell, swallow food, talk, or touch. The remains of the soldier were a living nightmare of war's hideous destructivity hidden from the world by the government. The book was suppressed during World War II and republished in 1959 and made into an award-winning motion picture in 1971. The narrative is the mind's inner dialogue, the pathos of total helplessness:

MOTHER

Mother where are you?
Hurry mother hurry hurry hurry and wake me up. I'm having a nightmare mother where are you? Hurry mother. I'm down here. Here in the darkness. Pick me up. Rock-abye baby. Now I lay me down to sleep. Oh mother hurry because I can't wake up. Over here mother. When the wind blows the cradle will rock. Hold me up high high.
Mother you've gone away and forgotten me. Here I am. I can't wake up mother. Wake me up. I can't move. Hold me. I'm scared. Oh mother sing to me and rub me and bathe me and comb my hair and wash out my ears and play with my toes and clap my hands together and blow my nose and kiss my eyes and mouth like I've seen you do with Elizabeth like you must have done with me. Then I will wake up and I'll never leave or be afraid or dream again.
Oh no.
I can't. I can't stand it. Scream. Move. Shake something. Make a noise any noise. I can't stand it. Oh no no no. Please, I can't. Please no. Somebody come. Help me. I can't lie here forever like this until maybe years from now I die. I can't. Nobody can. It isn't possible. ...
Oh please, oh oh please. No no no please no. Please. Not me.[1]

Max Cleland: Vietnam Triple Amputee

When I was working on my Vietnam study of combat nightmares at the San Antonio VA Hospital, Max Cleland was head of the Veterans Administration. He was a combat veteran who had lost both legs and one arm in a grenade explosion in Vietnam. After prolonged hospitalizations, surgeries, depression, and nightmares, he remade himself into a real-life model of strength and hope for the Vietnam veterans who then were

[1]Trumbo, Dalton. *Johnny Got His Gun*. New York: Citadel Press, 1991, pp. 84-86, 107-9.

usually ignored on the VA psychiatric services. Vietnam veterans were often used as scapegoats for the lost war by the public. There was no official diagnosis to make them legitimate VA psychiatric patients who would then be eligible for compensation for their mental trauma.

I observed that they were thought of as goldbricks after pensions they did not deserve. They were even called "malingerers." A mutual hostility grew between the VA and the Vietnam veterans, who were ignored by the mental health workers. Thus, recurrent catastrophic war nightmares, flashbacks, and depression tormented their lives. This was in the 1970s, before the diagnosis of posttraumatic stress disorder was officially recognized. VA psychiatrists ignored the nightmares and military records of Vietnam veterans. The treatment was medication, not talking and listening.

Max Cleland, over great opposition in the Washington bureaucratic Veterans Administration, created the Vet Centers, freestanding, autonomous centers staffed by Vietnam veterans for Vietnam veterans. Patient records were kept separate from the VA hospitals. These centers had a profoundly positive effect on the veterans who had been shattered by catastrophic combat experiences.

Max Cleland was helpful to me in my Vietnam project when I ran into hostile resistance by the chief of psychiatry and many of my peers among the psychiatric staff at the VA Hospital. When I finished my study, he read and commented on my manuscript, entitled *The Healing Nightmare*.[1]

Later, as president and director of the Institute for the Humanities at Salado, I invited Max to give a seminar and lecture at the institute on his life story, *Strong at the Broken Places*.[2] He was the highly popular secretary of state for Georgia, and soon thereafter, he became a United States senator from that state. I mentioned that I was writing this

[1]Wilmer, Harry A. "The Healing Nightmare: A Study of the War Dreams of Vietnam Combat Veterans" in *Quadrant*, Vol. 19 (Spring 1986), pp. 47-62.
[2]Cleland, Max. *Strong at the Broken Places: A Personal Story*. New York: Berkley Books, 1982.

book on silence during his seminar, which was recorded. This is what he had to say:

> I have a story to share with you about silence. It's a powerful story. It's real. About three weeks ago, I was in New York, and heard a general say, "When it's all over," he said, "I will remember the silences."
>
> It's funny you said "silence" today, because you did not know this story. When you said "silence," I said to myself, "Wow!"
>
> So this general said, "When it's all over, ... I will remember the silences – after, and before. ... The silences after I have given the order to attack, and they leave the room. I see their backs go out the door, and they shut the door. And I am alone in the silence. I know there are citizens out there, walking around, living their lives, planning their futures. They are buying a new home, planning to have kids. Their lives are short-lived. They will be sacrificed in the attack and they don't know it. And I am left alone in the silence. ... And then I remember the silences before the enemy attack. Just before the missiles come in. Just before the retribution is rendered. Just before the rocket goes off."
>
> And he said, "In the silences, I ask myself, 'Isn't there a better way?'" [Pause]
>
> And that was Yitzhak Rabin, ten days before the assassination.[1]

---

[1] Cleland, Max. Seminar at the Institute for the Humanities at Salado (Salado, Texas), November 19, 1995, transcript of tape recording.

It Is So, But the Prophesy Is Not Fulfilled

When C. G. Jung was interviewed in 1912 by a reporter from the *New York Times* following his lecture at Fordham University, he said:

> I find the greatest self-control in the world among the Americans – and I search for a cause. Why should there be so much self-control, I ask myself, in America, and I find an answer – brutality. I find a great deal of prudery. What is the cause, I ask, and I discover brutality. It is necessary – it makes life possible until you discover the brute and take real control of it. When you do that in America, then you will be the most emotional, the most temperamental, the most fully developed people in the world.[1]

America has nourished brutality in her soldiers in wars, because that is the nature of wars. This realization came to our American consciousness during the Vietnam War – our failure. More than one critic noted the resemblance to our war on the Indians. The American prudery led to citizens projecting their own murderous and cruel unconscious on the returning veterans. They offered no rites de sortie to prepare the returning Vietnam combat veterans for their reentry into a civilized society. We trained them to kill the North Vietnamese because they were "gooks," or subhuman objects.

At the time of the Persian Gulf War, President Bush celebrated "Rolling Thunder" as the end of the American Vietnam syndrome. It was a premature requiem. We didn't even call Vietnam a war, but a conflict. President Johnson declared war on poverty and crime, and did not win them either. Vietnam can be called an American unconscious shadow in company with our wars on the Indians and slavery. They may be past history but are still quite alive in our psyches and still affect

---

[1]McGuire, William, and R. F. C. Hull (Eds.) *Jung Speaking: Interviews and Encounters.* Princeton, N.J.: Princeton University Press, 1977, pp. 14-15 (citing a *New York Times* interview, Sunday, September 29, 1912).

our thinking and our prejudices. Someone said that the past is not dead – it is not even past.

Ares, the Greek god of war, was considered a blustering brutal coward, among that civilization's least likable gods. The Greeks favored Athena, the armed goddess of wisdom, whose wisdom always dominated her arms. Later, the Roman god of war, Mars, was exalted as military power and glory, and was one of the chief gods of the pantheon.[1] The war god business has not improved since then.

Deeply affected by hearing the Vietnam combat veterans tell me their war dreams at the Audie Murphy Veterans Administration in San Antonio, I asked for and was granted two years (1976-78) as a sabbatical from my ordinary clinical responsibilities to create a Vietnam veterans special study. At first, I was told that Vietnam was the past and I would be wasting my time, and that the study and treatment of war dreams were not according to the VA treatment program. That was my point, but I convinced the hospital director and chief of staff that the psychological treatment of Vietnam veterans might be a most important, otherwise ignored task.

I began seeing any Vietnam combat veteran who wanted to talk with me, and knew that I was particularly interested in war nightmares. Patients were referred to me from other wards in the hospital and from the Vet Center downtown, but mostly by hearing from another veteran. They often sought me because their nightmares were their main problem. The veterans were ignored or treated with pills to sleep or to cope with depression and anxiety. It is not surprising that many turned to alcohol or street drugs. That someone actually wanted to listen to their dreams was a new experience they were eager to test out. The fact that I was a full professor of psychiatry in a medical school with a good reputation and had established considerable trust with veterans on my VA ward for schizophrenic patients were helpful details.

---

[1]Evans, Bergen. *Dictionary of Mythology*. New York: Dell, 1972, p. 187.

I held a weekly dream seminar on the ward. One day a Vietnam veteran whom I will call Jose told the group a nightmare that had haunted him several times a week for six years. In the otherwise silent room, I suddenly felt transposed to the actual Vietnam combat experience as if I could hear and see it. This identification with the veteran was a powerful and alarming experience which I knew I had to pursue. I began seeing Jose several times a week. Mostly I listened and he told me his dreams and life story. Over time, his nightmare made dramatic changes. This was an important and unsuspected clue to me.

While I had been on active duty as a captain in the navy medical corps during the Korean War, I treated many veterans of that war and wrote a book on the subject.[1] I had never been under fire in actual combat, but knew the classic war nightmare was a dream reliving a catastrophic killing event. It was an unwished for return to a most terrible time, unlike any other dream known to psychiatry – predictable, recurrent, and without the changing hallucinatory effects of ordinary nightmares.

I discovered that analysts from Freud on had avoided analyzing or working with this unique category of dreams because it did not fit into the classical formulations of wish fulfillment, censorship, or Freud's libido theory. Jung, who did not buy these Freudian ideas, nevertheless wrote that one just had to wait them out, and they would die out. The trouble was, the nightmares were apt to continue for decades or a lifetime. I was told by Jungian analyst, Marie-Louise von Franz, in Zurich, about how Jung had worked with the war nightmare of a patient until it changed and then disappeared. This outcome was a possibility that I was to rediscover.

I began seeking other combat veterans and listening to their dreams: I interviewed 109 combat veterans for a minimum of three hours on two occasions. I saw some of them in

---

[1]Wilmer, Harry A. *Social Psychiatry in Action: A Therapeutic Community*. Springfield, IL.: Charles C. Thomas, 1958.

brief psychotherapy or analysis for months. When I reviewed all of their charts, there was not one in which a doctor had written a nightmare or combat experience. These men told me 459 different nightmares. Since they were recurrent, I only counted them once, unless there were additional different nightmares. Considering how often these dreams repeated for years, the study encompassed thousands of dreams.

In World War I, similar conditions were diagnosed as war neurosis or shell shock, in World War II as combat fatigue, and today, as posttraumatic stress disorder. Returning soldiers' war nightmares with terrible images, and waking in cold drenching sweats, have been recorded since the earliest battles. Warriors have told epic heroic or tragic stories, but mostly have remained silent about their worst combat experiences.

Jose, age twenty-eight, was a sergeant in Vietnam from 1971 to 1972. His nightmare was as vivid as if it had been recorded on video or cinema verité. It was the story of the time he volunteered to be the point man on a search-and-destroy operation, just a week before his one-year tour of duty was finished. Jose led seventeen recently arrived soldiers to their death in an ambush. Only Jose had escaped and watched the trapped men from a foxhole above the ravine. He saw the dead, heard the wounded screaming, and saw the Vietcong going systematically from one survivor to another – shooting each one in the head.

Later, he escaped from the area and returned to the base camp. Jose returned in the morning with a squad, and found all the men decapitated, their heads placed on punji sticks and smeared with feces. Jose was despondent and overcome with feelings of guilt and rejection. He told me he felt he had been "banished." Since his year was up and Jose was unable to function, he was sent back home.

He was repeatedly hospitalized, while he drank excessively and used barbiturates, marijuana, and heroin. His family life was a disaster, and he lived in dread that something terrible would happen to his children. Doctors told him that his nightmare would go away: "Just take the medicine and come back in six weeks for a follow-up." Then someone told him a psychiatrist downstairs was interested in Vietnam nightmares. He knocked at my door. My treatment of Jose was mostly patient listening and very few interpretations. I heard the same nightmare over and over again. I told him we would find some meaning in his dreams and his war experience. He was skeptical but hopeful, and eager to see me. I have reported elsewhere how his dreams changed and then lost all of their power, but the Vietnam combat stories I tell in this chapter are to emphasize the monstrous noise and seeming impossibility of achieving peace and quiet to end their torment. It was the silence – or listening – that brought about whatever healing was possible.[1]

Another patient had this short recurrent dream:

I can hear the awful sound of an incoming rocket, but just before it strikes the motor cuts off and there is silence. I don't know where it is coming from or where it is going until it explodes and I wake up.

A marine sergeant, who had served in Korea, was badly wounded in Vietnam. This is his repeated nightmare:

There is a big flash and everybody is hurting and crying for the corpsman, "Medic! Medic!" Then everybody is kinda lying there hearing the helicopters come in. An army lieutenant is walking across the knoll with no foot. It was blown off. I hear him getting aboard the damn helicopter dragging the bone across the steel deck and – damn that hurts to look at. He didn't even know what was happening. I wake up sweating and say, "Oh shit! That happened all over again." I get a real bad headache then. I just lay there. I feel like somebody has put an axe between my ears.

[1]Wilmer, Harry A. "The Healing Nightmare," Chapter 6 in *Trauma and Dreams* edited by Deirdre Barrett. Cambridge, Mass.: Harvard University Press, 1996, pp. 85-99.

Another veteran's nightmare:

There is no sound. I am looking into the jungle. People open their mouths and nothing comes out, like the TV with the sound turned off. Then suddenly the sound comes on full blast. That doesn't last long.

And still another veteran's nightmare:

We get into this little village about six miles north of Da Nang. A bunch of little children are running toward us. The captain yells, "Fire!" When we fire, they explode. They were loaded with grenades tied to them. They didn't disintegrate – they just blew into pieces.

On Not Being Able to Talk

I was scheduled to give a university lecture on my Vietnam study in a small auditorium. All of the chairs and spaces along the walls and steps were filled with medical students, psychiatric residents, psychologists, university faculty, VA staff, Vet Center staff, and friends. I was unusually apprehensive, even though I felt I would face a receptive audience with positive feelings for me. I also was aware that the young people admired what I was doing, but some senior psychiatric faculty members were ambivalent, jealous, or indifferent. Moreover, I was about to give a speech on an unpopular, politically hot subject – the Vietnam War and the veterans.

Standing on the podium, I looked out over a sea of friendly waiting faces. Then I spoke without reading my paper for about ten minutes, when an odd feeling of estrangement slowly crept over me until I felt tearful and could not speak a word. It was as if I had slipped into a quicksand of muteness. Fighting back the tears, again I scanned the audience and sensed that they were withdrawing in a kind of benevolent reaction to my grief and pain. The small auditorium was now filled with rows of expressionless faces.

It must have been thirty seconds or more before I could utter a word. Although they seemed open and relieved, I was now about to say things that they did not want to hear. I had not lost the sense of a basically friendly audience, and I gradually regained my composure and resumed talking. The audience and I were both relieved.

During the interval when I was speechless, I was struck by the realization that combat veterans cannot or will not speak about their personal war horrors because people do not want to hear, see, or listen, because disbelievers do not trust the messenger, or do not even care. A Vietnam veteran who was in the audience said to me after the lecture that I was their "point man." I was not only presenting psychological evidence, I was pleading a case as close to the truth as I saw it.

The situation made me recall the story of Anthony Cooper, a British member of the House of Commons who prepared a speech in favor of a bill on human rights to abolish the law stating that a prisoner accused of high treason was not allowed to be represented by counsel unless a special matter of law was stated by the court. There was strong opposition to abolishing the law. Cooper stood up in the House to read his speech but became so agitated that he was unable to go on. The speaker of the House, seeing his confusion, told him to take his time and not be discouraged. Cooper recovered and spoke these words:

> Mr. Speaker, if I, who rose only to give my opinion on a bill now pending, am so confounded that I am unable to express the least part of which I proposed to say, what must be the condition of a man, who, without any assistance whatever, is obliged to plead for his life, whilst under the dreadful apprehension of being deprived of it?

He sat down, and the bill to abolish the prohibition of counsel was passed.[1]

[1]Source unknown.

It has been said by theologians that the highest communication between God and humankind occurs in silence. That was not the way Elie Wiesel heard God in Auschwitz. In 1945, Wiesel was liberated from the concentration camp at Buchenwald. At that time, he made a vow of silence for ten years that he would not speak out about his experience as a prisoner at Auschwitz or of the fate of six million Jews. When he finally broke his silence, he had trouble finding a publisher for his book because of the depressive subject. When *Night* was published in 1958, few people wanted to read about the Holocaust. In 1986, Wiesel was awarded the Nobel Peace Prize.

Wiesel's journey to the concentration camps began as the train arrived:

> Suddenly we heard terrible screams: "Jews, look through the window! Flames! Look!
> And as the train stopped, we saw that flames were gushing out of a tall chimney into the black sky. ... We looked at the flames in the darkness. There was an abominable odor floating in the air. ... In front of us flames. In the air that smell of burning flesh. It must have been about midnight. We had arrived – at Birkenau, reception center for Auschwitz. ...
> Never shall I forget that night, the first night in camp that turned my life into one dark night, seven times cursed and seven times sealed. Never shall I forget that smoke. Never shall I forget the little faces of the children, whose bodies I saw turned into wreaths of smoke beneath a silent blue sky.
> Never shall I forget those flames which consumed my faith forever.
> Never shall I forget that nocturnal silence which deprived me, for all eternity, of the desire to live. Never shall I forget those moments which murdered my God and my soul and turned my dreams to dust. Never shall I forget those

things, even if I am condemned to live as long as God Himself. Never.[1]

The Seventh Seal is Silence

When the Lamb opened the seventh seal, there was silence in heaven for about half an hour.

The Revelation to John, 8:1

Everything in heaven came to a stop for thirty minutes. The silence was in Heaven, not on earth. Heaven went to sleep and woke up a half an hour later to the sounds of the galloping hoofbeats of four horses, the cries of the saints, the upheaval of the earthquake, and the hymns of praise in Heaven followed by the seven trumpets.

Billy Smith, Presbyterian minister at Salado, tells me that this description relates to John's seven letters to the seven churches in Asia Minor to prepare them to face the imminent ordeals in the life and death battle of the church. The scrolls were closed with seven seals. Their contents were mysterious. God will not break the seals of His scroll and put its contents into action because human destiny and all creation are achieved by humanity. The Lamb alone is worthy to open the seven seals. After the six seals are opened, the seventh is silence.

In 1982, Elie Wiesel lamented:

Ancient sages have told us that it takes three years to learn how to talk – and seventy years how to be silent. ...

For the poet, the artist, the mystic, the survivor, silence has many facets, zones, and shades. Silence has its own texture, its own spheres, its own archeology. It has its own contradictions as well. The silence of the victim is one thing, that of the killer, another. There is a creative silence, there is a murderous silence. To a perceptive human being

[1]Wiesel, Elie. *Night*. New York: Bantam Books, 1986, p. 25 ff. & p. 32.

the universe is never silent – but there exists a universal silence and only perceptive human beings are aware of it.[1]

Home of the Brave

ACT II, Scene 1: Hospital Room, The Pacific Base

DOCTOR: Coney ... Remember when Finch was shot?
CONEY: Yeah. I remember.
DOCTOR: When you heard that shot and saw he was hit, what did you think of?
CONEY: I ... I got a bad feeling.
DOCTOR: But what did you think of, Coney? At that moment what went through your head?
CONEY: I didn't want to leave him.
DOCTOR: What did you think of at that instant, Coney?[2]

It was August 1952 at a small private mental hospital in Belmont, California. I was looking at a man who was screaming, "You're killing me!" Soon he was unable to speak. Later when he could speak, no one would believe him.

From 1945-1949, I had my psychiatric training at the Mayo Clinic. Patients who could not afford a private hospital room ($14.00 a day) were warehoused in the country in an enormous state hospital with barred windows. For one month, I was assigned to the Rochester (Minnesota) State Hospital and given one hundred patients to look after.

There were huge open wards with beds packed one next to the other. During the day, the patients sat on rows of wooden benches along the wall – many tied with leather restraints, some stiff in straitjackets. Other patients had torn their clothes off and roamed nakedly around the room. Catatonic

---

[1]Wiesel, Elie. "The School of Works" in *Somewhere a Master: Further Hasidic Portraits and Legends*. New York: Summit Books, 1982, pp. 179 ff. & 200-201.
[2]Laurents, Arthur. *Home of the Brave: Players Edition*. Dramatists Play Service, 1945, pp. 34-35.

schizophrenic patients stood all day in fixed, odd poses – like statues. Episodic violence and injury to patients and staff occurred. Patients remained locked up for long periods. Some were confined to open or closed wards for life. If it was not a snake pit, it certainly resembled one. I vowed to myself that if ever there were a chance to change such conditions, I would do it. I did not feel the need to be a hero, but rather utter despair at the inhuman conditions.

In the 1940s, there were no effective medications, only time, electroshock therapy, insulin coma, and lobotomy at the Rochester State Hospital. There were few psychiatrists, and poorly paid, untrained technicians.

When I left the Mayo Clinic and went to start a department of psychiatry at the Palo Alto Clinic in California, a few reforms were already in motion and I had great hope. Almost miraculously, by the last year of my psychiatric fellowship at Mayo, a movement to humanize the state hospitals in Minnesota started. On Halloween 1949, Governor Luther Youngdahl set a torch to a great pile of all the mechanical restraints from all the state hospitals brought to Hastings State Hospital for a bonfire celebration.

In another decade, there were bold efforts to change psychiatric institutions. I was a part of that. Yet by the mid-1950s, with the arrival of new effective drugs, the movement toward more humane hospital care was coming to a halt. Drugs took the limelight and the money from humanistic and psychological care. Psychiatrists led the cry for "deinstitutionalization" to close down the state hospitals and start community mental health services. State hospitals shrunk, were ignored, and starved for money. Underpaid, demoralized doctors and technicians reverted to their custodial mentality.

Too-lengthy hospitalization was replaced by too-brief, creating the revolving door phenomenon. Patients took their long-term care in repeated, short, small doses. Human continuity and responsibility atrophied. The idealistic, extremely expensive, community-based Mental Health-Mental Retardation program (MHMR) gradually deteriorated and today is a shadow of what it was meant to be.

The inspiration for change to a balanced, humane and psychopharmacological care was sacrificed on the altar of technology. The thinking was about expediency, and statistical and economic factors. The humanities became the sacrificial goat on the altar.

Savages Attack: Who is Possessed by Demons?

I have kept a diary since 1940. I am going to relate an entry made on August 16, 1952:

After a busy day seeing patients at the Palo Alto Clinic, I drove to the Alexander Sanatorium in the village of Belmont, about twenty miles north, to see the two patients I had hospitalized there. I arrived at 6:30 p.m., parked my car in the wood-shaded driveway, and walked across the beautiful grounds to the building where my patients were.

As I passed another building on my right, I was startled to hear the sound of shattering glass on a cement walkway by a door. It sounded like glass wind-chimes gone wild in a sudden gale.

For a moment, I froze. Two patients walked by me on the sidewalk. One said jokingly, "Some stupid attendant dropped another dinner tray."

I walked closer to the place from where the sound had come. On the concrete walk beneath a glass door lay a metal gooseneck desk lamp surrounded by shards of glass. There was a large hole in a glass pane of the door, about the size of a man's head. The door was locked, so naturally I looked into the hole.

I will never forget what I saw. About ten feet from my eyes, a very large man in hospital pyjamas was held to the floor by four white-jacketed attendants. Another attendant struck the patient's head with his fist. There were several people in the noisy room, nurses and a young doctor whom I recognized, standing aside, just watching.

An attendant saw me staring through the glass hole in the door, rushed over, and stood with his back blocking my porthole view. My utter bewilderment became furious anger as I realized that I was involved. The thought of walking away never occurred to me. Adrenaline sent my heart beating wildly. I entered the building through the side door and walked to the open door of the patient's room from which I could hear the commotion, mumbled talk, and – I thought – gasps.

A nurse rushed past me down the hall carrying a syringe and vials of medication. She saw me. She recognized me. She went into the room without closing the door. I followed her and stood in the doorway both angry and frightened. An attendant saw me, and yelled to the nurse, "What's he doing here?" She replied, "He's Dr. Wilmer." The young psychiatrist who was watching the beating looked at me with a blank, indifferent expression. He said nothing.

I stood my ground silently, paralyzed in disbelief as I saw an attendant garrote the patient's neck with a hospital towel bearing the orange markings of the sanitorium. He twisted it. The patient's ashen grey, sweating head and lips turned to a deadly cyanotic purple. Gasping for breath, he managed to cry out, "You're killing me!"

The nurse gave him an injection in the arm at the direction of the doctor. The body soon became limp, then unconscious. The whole event seemed surreal. The attendants lifted the limp body onto the bed. Then they strapped him onto a gurney and wheeled past me. I could see the fresh red marks of a fist on the right side of his head and on his eye. The gurney was accompanied by an entourage of two technicians, the nurse, and the doctor – and me.

Instantly I began to be outraged by my silence. Why had I stood there like a passive idiot? What could I – what should I – have done? The gurney went down a street to the lower level of the main building, through a door that I knew led to the

place where electroshock therapy was administered. So, that's
what they were going to do! It would wipe out his memory of
what had just happened. He would wake up dazed and
confused.

For a moment, I stood outside the door, aware that I had
not the slightest idea why this patient was in the hospital, or
what had led up to the assault. I had been the accidental silent
observer.

While driving home, I became agitated, angry, and afraid.
Supper was tasteless and I was withdrawn from Jane and the
children. What could I say? I went to bed early but did not
sleep. At midnight I got up, went into my study, and typed a
letter about what I had seen to Dr. Tallman in Sacramento,
director of the Department of Mental Health of the state of
California. He was a psychiatrist whom I knew and trusted. It
was a clumsy report of the facts without feelings. I did not yet
know enough about the entire case, but I had to write what I
had seen and experienced – outrageous physical abuse of a
patient.

I tore up the letter of description and wrote a brief sum-
mary followed by an expression of my feelings. Almost to my
surprise, it came out in free verse. I edited it many times:

> It is late at night.
> I cannot sleep.
> I still see his terror-stricken face,
> A death-like ashen grey mask.
>
> His neck garroted by a towel,
> Twisted by a fist behind the vertebrae.
> Restrained, he had thrashed out, struck out.
> Now he was going limp.
>
> The now-quieter, senseless man,
> Whipped, beaten,
> Kicked, mauled, kneed,
> Pummeled, slugged, choked, cried out.

With the volcanic force
Of retaliation, fear and brutality,
Men afraid of being hurt or killed
Beat and throttled him till he was unconscious.

I had seen through a shattered glass
This cruel, cowardly, stupid deed,
Done in the presence of doctor and nurses.
Then electroconvulsive treatment – the *coup de grâce*.

If I speak out, loud and clear,
I will remind the mentally ill of their worst fear:
Cruel treatment in psychiatric hospitals.
But, dare I not speak out?

Oh God! I cannot erase this memory.
With my eyes closed, it goes on replaying.
What is my responsibility to this man,
To my patients, to my profession, to myself?

With feelings so intense, I cannot speak
Or write except in this poetic form.
I will mail it to Tallman in the morning.
Will there be relief?

The next day I was allowed to review this patient's chart
and discovered that he had been admitted several days earlier
for psychiatric evaluation concerning a worker's compensation claim for physical and mental consequences of an accident. There were no symptoms or diagnoses that would have
warranted the emergency electroshock treatment. I was not
opposed to electroshock for intransigent depression, but was
alarmed when it was misused.

I thought that they had given him this treatment to blur his
memory, to discredit him as a witness or observer, and that
such drastic treatment would be seen as evidence that he was
violent and uncontrollable. He had been punished. The young
psychiatrist who was a new assistant medical director, cover-
ing for doctors whose patients were in the hospital, would do

everything to cover himself and discredit me if it came to a hearing. I could expect that my reputation might now be in serious jeopardy.

I went to talk with the assistant medical director who had been on the job for one month. He was alone in his office. I asked him what had happened and why he had participated. He answered with a candor of innocence, "To hold my job." After a moment, I said, "I am deeply disturbed by what I saw and what I have learned from the patient's chart." To my disgust, he looked me in the eye and with a patronizing air responded, "Are you?" I ended the interview. The next day, I transferred my patients from the sanatorium to Stanford Hospital, and the young doctor said, "Are you transferring them to get psychological testing?"

Because of this event, the attendants were fired. I spoke with the physician chief of staff, who listened politely and was noncommittal. On September 7, 1953, I received the following letter from his assistant chief of staff:

> We want you to accept our apology for having discommended [sic] you when there was an incident with one of our patients about two weeks ago. ... I know you will appreciate the occasional difficulty a mental hospital will encounter in dealing with a belligerent or negativistic patient who may have temporarily eluded control. Such, essentially, were the circumstances in this case. It is regrettable, of course, that such an incident should occur, and naturally we do our best to avoid such an event. However, it is also regrettable that this incident was intruded on your notice. And we are indeed sorry for any inconvenience we may have caused you or your patients.[1]

At this time, I was in psychoanalysis with an analyst in whom I had great confidence. He happened to be president of the American Psychoanalytic Association, but because he was out of town, I did not have an opportunity to analyze the

[1]Personal communication.

situation and my reaction. I was eager to see him on his return because I had decided that I would bring this case to a formal complaint and hearing. Dr. Tallman had encouraged me to do this because, while these things do happen, it hardly ever happens that a reputable outside psychiatrist is a witness.

I felt it was a moral decision whether to testify. Psychoanalysts in those days were supposed to be noncommittal and neutral. I was surprised, perplexed, and even relieved when my analyst reminded me that public hearings of this nature would have sensational media coverage in San Francisco and the Bay area. Because I was just beginning my practice, he thought it would be preferable if I were to spend my energies and time in analyzing rather than getting into political turmoil. I was hurt, however, when he said, "This would happen to you! – and when I was away." Was I that special and in such need of a father?

The next day, I wrote to Tallman telling him that I would not make a formal written complaint. I go into these specific memories because The Alexander Episode was a major determining factor in my future career in psychiatry. My mother always preached that it was not necessary to fight. My father wanted me to be a doctor so that in war I would be helping, not killing. Now, I wanted to do battle. Consequently, I bore a heavy feeling of guilt for years. I felt that when I had a chance to stand up, I chickened out and spent my time analyzing my Oedipal complex lying on my back on the couch.

Again, I swore to myself that if I ever had a chance to control a psychiatric ward or hospital, I would create such a program that violent abuse would not happen. I had that opportunity when I was in the navy during the Korean War a few years later. War and savagery go hand in hand. It begins with individual incidents.

We are told that whenever an unknown Bororo arrived at a village, he was subjected to a thorough examination, the aim of which was to find out whether or not he was carrying any object of interest. If he was, he was warmly welcomed; otherwise he was murdered.[1]

Wartime Secret

For thirty-five years, the British government kept secret its knowledge of plans to bomb Coventry, England, on November 14, 1940. In 1982, historian William Stevenson wrote a best-selling book entitled *A Man Named Intrepid*, the code name for an unknown heroic spy named William Ste*ph*enson. He was a member of the highly secret intelligence center for cryptography at Bletchley, England, where a machine called Ultra was created. With this device, they had broken the secret German military code, a fact that the Germans never knew throughout World War II.

During the first week of November 1940, Hitler's order to destroy Coventry was decoded. Within minutes, Winston Churchill had this information. He faced a dreadful decision, because if he ordered an evacuation of Coventry, the Nazis would have known their code was broken, and the value of Ultra would have been lost forever. The message was kept secret. Exactly at the scheduled hour on the morning of November 14, Luftwaffe bombers leveled Coventry, killing thousands of people and destroying the fourteenth-century cathedral of Saint Michael.[2]

Max Picard wrote:

> The cathedrals are deserted today, just as silence is deserted. They have become museums of silence, but they are all inter-related, cathedral with cathedral, silence with silence. They stand like ichthyosauri of silence, no longer understood by any one. It was inevitable that they should

[1]Lévi-Strauss, Claude. *The Raw and the Cooked: Introduction to a Science of Mythology*. New York: Harper & Row, 1969, p. 52, fn. 6.
[2]Stevenson, William. *A Man Named Intrepid: The Secret War*. New York: Ballantine, 1982, pp. 164-65.

be bombarded in the war: absolute noise, shooting at absolute silence.[1]

[1]Picard, *World of Silence*, p. 169.

6

MA

This morning on my walk, the songs in the trees were unusually clear and distinct as one bird sang to another in different trees. It was a warm spring Texas day and I was being entertained by a chorale of invisible singers up in the sky. As I walked along the path winding through the large oak trees, it seemed that I was hearing the word-songs in an almost familiar language – words imitating birds, melodies in crisp recitatives.

I looked up suddenly as a scarlet cardinal swooped down from the upper leafy branches of a live oak tree, sailing close beside my leg, then banking off into a nearby hedge. Its flight swayed like a swift breeze, barely missing the closely inter-twining branches and twigs, as the red spot disappeared into the greenness. I marveled at its flight and close encounter, and said to myself, "Of course, that is the miracle of the BIRD-MA!"

It need hardly be said that my cat Mitten, walking ahead with his nose scenting the ground, was oblivious to the bird. I remembered that someone had given him a water cup with the inscription "Bird Lover" on it. Just now, the song and flight of that bright red bird-ma had captured my imagination.

The Japanese Word MA

The key to Japanese culture lies in the asymmetrical intervals: spacing, rhythms of writing, designing, music, dancing, the arts. Above all, it lies in the ability to see and feel space. The MA perceived as an area of change – of hues, brightness, shape – becomes symbolized in all sorts of gestures, idioms, etc., throughout the cultural and practical arts, and comes to be symbolized in the area of freedom.[1]

Practically every aspect of Japanese life asserts the integrity of the interval perceived as meaningful pauses, says Edmund Carpenter, who explains that:

In contrast, practically every aspect of Western life asserts the exclusive integrity of things, objects, masses. Spaces between objects aren't perceived as integers at all; the ideal in technological machines which yield power, and in Art & Life as well, is to negate and nullify intervals into rhythmical, balanced, symmetrical patterns, all exactly alike.[2]

In Japanese Shinto sacred places, the MA space is designed to be open, empty, and pure in preparation for coming and going. There are MA-like spaces within shrines, caves, rock-created spaces, churches, synagogues, mosques, and homes.

I chose to use the word MA to suggest what we know as silence. The word has a relational meaning – with, among, and between. The first time this concept came vividly to my mind was when I saw a Monet painting exhibit, "The Water Lilies," at the New Orleans Art Museum.

"Everyone discusses [my art] and pretends to understand, as if it were necessary to understand, when it is simply

---

[1]Lanier, Emilio, cited by Edmund Carpenter on "Interval" in *They Became What They Beheld*. New York: Ballantine, 1970.
[2]Carpenter, Edmund. *They Became What They Beheld*. New York: Ballantine, 1970.

necessary to love," wrote Claude Monet in 1925. Monet lived and painted in the rural village of Giverny by a lily pond over which he built a Japanese bridge. For the last three decades of his life, he painted large-scale impressionistic canvases of water lilies which are related to the lotuses, sacred symbols in ancient cultures. As I looked at these huge canvases – dotted with water lilies, alone or in clumps, separated by light and open spaces of the pond with its reflection of the sky – I thought, "MA!" They were drawn in the spirit of the Japanese print where the intervening spaces gave meaning to the objects.

Monet wrote:

> Perhaps my originality boils down to my capacity as a hypersensitive receptor, and to the expediency of a shorthand by means of which I project onto a canvas, as if onto a screen, impressions registered on my retina. If you absolutely must find an affiliation for me, select the Japanese of olden times; their rarefied taste has always appealed to me; and I sanction the implications of their aesthetic that evokes a presence by means of a shadow and the whole by means of a fragment.[1]

MA in America – Not

The American grammar of silence is noise, conflicts, and plugged gaps. There is no English expression comparable to MA. The widespread hunger for the mysterious, spiritual, and mystical experiences is blurred by obsessive rational and scientific opinions. We are addicted to the tube and dogmatic, vociferous fast-speak. Our experts, once given the air, pontificate with answers to questions and predicaments to which there are no enduring answers.

[1]Stuckey, Charles F. *Monet: Water Lilies*. New York: Park Lane, 1988, p. 18.

Our TV personalities espouse glib, dogmatic, or attempted great thoughts. They rewrite past histories in the "if only" genre, and foresee the unknowable future. All this on baited breath. When faced with the awesome imminence of silent pauses, they are at no loss for words that erupt out of their vocal cord spigots. MA becomes trendy clichés:

MA becomes: On the one hand ... On the other hand. ...

MA becomes: A level playing field.

MA becomes: Having said that. ...

MA becomes: At this point in time. ...

MA becomes: Statistics and opinion polls show. ...

MA becomes: You know. ...

MA becomes: What you are really saying is. ...

MA becomes: Of course, you have a right to your opinion.

MA becomes: Believe me. ...

MA becomes: Now for the latest news. ...

MA becomes: Etcetera, etcetera, etcetera.

Eric was a patient whose mother gave him the silent treatment. He said she seemed to him to be hiding something until he spoke the magic words as she waited behind a wall of stony silence. Eric compared the magic words to "Open Sesame!" Eric's authoritarian father acted as if he knew all the answers and hid behind a cloak of sham humility. My patient would wake up almost every morning, saying to himself, "You think you know everything" or "You don't know for sure!" He would sometimes repeat the same words, surprised at odd times during the day. He asked me, "Where in the world do these repetitive voices come from?" Eric thought he might be talking to someone else. I asked him for any association.

Eric replied immediately, "As a matter of fact, I was listening to Dr. Joyce Brothers yesterday on her pop radio psychotherapy show when she got a call from a woman who was at her wit's end trying to manage her obstreperous little boy of ten. The mother began to tell of her anguish and how she was trying to cope. Dr. Brothers cut in with a barrage of 'No! No! No! No! No!,' followed by a tirade of criticism, advice, and jack-in-the-box pop-up answers. It would all turn out really simple if mother would follow doctor's orders. Dr. Brothers' 'No! No! No! No! No!' were the magic words of a witch stirring the brew in a caldron over a fire. 'Throw in some newts, an eye of walleyed pike, and the head of a frog, and stir quickly. Do not inhale.'"

It reminds me of musician John Cage's great line from his book, *Silence*: "I have nothing to say, and I'm saying it."[1]

We make noise. Americans are addicted to the mechanical, industrial metaphor of "making." People moving up the ladder are on the make. Ambitious people want to make a million or a billion. People speak of making a killing, call themselves self-made, tell others not to make waves. Young men make women. Sometimes we must make time, make a living, make love, make babies. We make friends, and make fools of ourselves.

A pop culture speaks of making souls. Many religious, mystical, and spiritual people are deep in the lofty business of soul making. It is popular for therapists, especially Jungian analysts, to characterize their work as soul making. They seriously believe that they are gifted at making souls. I can understand the idea of loss of soul, or its return or redemption, but it seems to me grossly inflated to propose that the souls can be manufactured by analysts.

You might argue that my opinion is flawed by taking literally the metaphor of "making." Have I confused the sacred with the profane, or have I identified a significant point that has been glossed over and now requires discussion? Is our work as analysts to free silent spaces for listening from the flood of verbiage so that the soul may enter consciousness?

It is acceptable to ask for one minute of silence in remembrance of someone who has died, making the point that words cannot express our deepest feelings. Thinking technologically, we have created an artificial silence as a product to be inserted into the stream of words or noise. Thinking psychologically, we have moved to preverbal, primitive existence.

[1]Cage, *Silence*, p. 51.

The silence of which I write, however, cannot be made because it cannot be counted, weighed, or measured. In short, while it matters a great deal, it is not matter. It is not an object, territory, or property. It cannot be patented, captured, eaten, or killed. Because one cannot sell, buy, or place a monetary value on silence, it is worthless in the material, scientific world.

One attributes a negative value to ambivalent silence. Edgar Allan Poe wrote a short story entitled "Silence – A Fable," in which the demon summons his ultimate power, saying:

> Then I grew angry and curse with the curse of silence, the river and the lilies, the wind and the forest, and the heaven and the thunder, and the sighs of the water lilies. And they became accursed. ... immediately the characters on the rock turn to silence, and the man, his face wan with terror, rushes away.[1]

I may want to sell the idea of MA to the reader, but no one could sell MA, which is a priceless treasure. When we move from English to Japanese, we find that the word MA refers to the interval between, regarded as a positive element in all the arts rather than the absence of sound or image. MA is the silent empty space in painting, music, speech, and between things. It refers to the signal importance of empty spaces in human existence. The word MA is a Thing-Word standing for No-Thing.

MA Is Sometimes Ma

In Samuel Beckett's novel, *Molly*, Moran calls his mother Mag, and explains:

[1]Ward, J. A. *American Silences: The Realm of James R. Walker, Evans and Edward Hopper*. Baton Rouge, La.: Louisiana State University Press, 1985, pp. 11, 20, 26.

I call her Mag because for me, without knowing why, the
letter *g* abolished the syllable Ma, and as if it were spat on,
better than any other letter would have done. At the same
time I satisfied a deep and doubtless unacknowledged
need, the need to have a Ma, that is a mother and proclaim
it audibly.[1]

Crafted MA

Good writers, therapists, analysts, actors, actresses, public
speakers, and vocal performers of any sort use words, nonverbal gestures, and carefully crafted silences because they work.
At best, listeners are spellbound, which in turn affects the one
who is performing. It is a form of mutual empathy, but not
quite genuine empathy because it boils down to a technique.
Like the actor who said, "Once you can fake honesty, you have
it made."

Anyone who is planning to give a talk can change an
ordinary speech into a brilliant, successful presentation by
mastering the MA-business. John Wayne put it this way: "Talk
low, talk slow, and don't say too much."[2] Mark Twain said,
"The right word may be effective, but no word was ever as
effective as a rightly timed silence."[3]

Twain also wrote:

> When a man is reading on the platform, he soon realizes
> that there is one powerful gun in his battery of artifices
> that he can't work with an effect proportionate to its
> caliber: that is the pause – that impressive silence, that
> eloquent silence, that geometrically progressive silence
> which often achieves a desired effect where no combina-
> tion of words howsoever felicitous could accomplish. The

---

[1]Beckett, Samuel. *Molly* in *Three Novels by Samuel Beckett*. New York: Grove
Press, 1965, p. 17.
[2]Wayne, John. Source unknown.
[3]Twain, Mark. "Introductions" in *Speeches*, 1923.

pause is not much use to the man who is reading ...
Because he cannot know what the exact length of it ought
to be; he is not the one to determine the measurement – the
audience must do that for him. He must perceive by their
faces when the pause has reached its proper length ... – the
faces tell him when to end the pause. For one audience the
pause will be short, for another a little longer.[1]

A feature article on the death of Japanese composer, Toru
Takemitsu, in the *Dallas Morning News* of March 3, 1996, said
that he was reserved but polite, and that long pauses were as
characteristic of his conversation as they were of his music.
He wrote the music for the films *Ran* and *Woman in the Dunes*.
His composition, "Water Music," consisted of sounds of water
dripping, arranged into a quiet haunting work, and the words
were merely the sounds of a man and woman repeating the
Japanese word *ai* (love). The Japanese television documentary
four days after his death noted the importance he placed on
silence, and quoted Takemitsu: "It has been demonstrated that
dolphins communicated not by their gibbering voices but by
the various intervals of silence between the sound they emit –
a provocative discovery."[2]

The Significance of MA in Japanese Culture

It was my good fortune to spend a month with Japanese
analyst, Osamu Kuramitsu, in Salado in 1976. Here is what he
told me about MA:

> The Japanese word MA is based on a Chinese ideograph
> made by two components. One is composed of two poles
> and is pronounced "Mon," which means "Gate." The other

[1]Twain, Mark. *On Writing and Publishing.* New York: Book of the Month
Club, 1994, pp. 27-28.
[2]Chism, Olin. "Takemitsu and Gould: A Final Note" in *Dallas Morning News*
(March 3, 1996).

MA

is set between the poles, pronounced "Hi," and means "Sun" is located between two poles, so that the letter MA means something important between.

This sometimes suggests nothingness, like the beats between notes of music, the period between incidents and the comfortable distance between people, or in Noh Theater which is sometimes called "the art of MA."

MA is so important in Japanese culture, that if you lose MA in daily life you are a fool. (MA NUKE = losing MA – means fool.) If you wish to say "You got here just in time" or "It is very useful," say "MA NI AU" meaning "It meets MA."

The Japanese began to use the letter MA about one hundred years ago when Western culture was introduced into Japan. I imagine that our ancestors felt the need to add MA to express the concepts of Time, Space, and Human Beings. Previously in traditional culture, Time, Space, and Human Beings contained adequate MA, but in the beginning of the twentieth century there was the danger of losing MA, and missing important intervals, silence, and space between.[1]

Richard Pilgrim wrote that the MA interval between two or more special or temporal things and events (such as a gap, opening, or space) takes on a relational meaning – standing in, with, among, or between. The Chinese character that is the written word MA is an opening through which light shines, and the function of MA is precisely to let the light shine through.

Pilgrim wrote:

The word, therefore, carries both objective and subjective meaning: that is, MA is not only "something" within objective, descriptive reality but also signifies particular modes of experience. ... The latter usage is the point at which MA becomes a religio-aesthetic paradigm and being about the collapse of distinctive (objective) worlds, and even time and space itself. ... Therefore although MA may be objectively located at intervals in space and time, ultimately it transcends this and expresses a deeper level; indeed, it takes us to the boundary situation at the edge of thinking and the edge of a process of locating things by naming and distinguishing. ... The word MA at first seems vague, but it is the multiplicity of meanings and at the same time the conciseness of the single word that makes MA a unique conceptual term, one without parallel in other languages.

> Such a lot of snow
> that to do snow-viewing
> there's no place to go.[2]

[1]Kuramitsu, Osamu. Personal conversation with Harry Wilmer, Salado, Texas, 1997.
[2]Anonymous (late eighteenth century) in *An Introduction to Haiku* by Harold G. Henderson. Garden City, N.Y.: Doubleday Anchor Books, 1958, p. 126.

MA, intervals between, silence as empty space directs our attention to the process of emptying one's mind in meditation, of efforts to stop obsessive thinking that keep the mind from being at peace. This is a mighty task for Americans, but an ancient practice in the Far East (for example, the Zen philosophy of No-Mind). D. T. Suzuki describes this phenomenon in a way that one could substitute the word *silence* for the *emptiness*:

> Emptiness constantly falls within our reach; it is always with us and in us, and conditions all our knowledge, all our deeds, and is our life itself. It is only when we attempt to pick it up and hold it forth as something before our eyes that it eludes us, frustrates all our efforts, and vanishes like vapour. We are ever lured toward it, but it proves a will-o'-the-wisp.[1]

The Tao

Tao or Taoism, an ancient Chinese religion called The Way or The Middle Way or Parting of the Way, taught that empty space (or nothing) makes objects useful. According to ancient Chinese legend, the sage Lao-Tzu at the age of 160 grew so disgusted with the decay of the Chou dynasty due to the warring nations that he left the Middle Kingdom to travel West and find tranquillity.

War was no longer thought to be noble, and the killing was no longer directed against only armies but now against civilians as well. Chivalry was not practiced anymore. Warfare had become cruel savagery. The vanquished were killed and no longer spared. Cities were put to the sword. Atrocities and unrelenting reprisals destroyed civilization. Soldiers in one state were paid off only when they presented the paymaster with the severed heads of the enemy. Some chiefs boiled the

[1]Suzuki, D. T. *Zen Buddhism*. Garden City, N.Y.: Doubleday Anchor Books, 1956, p. 191.

bodies of those they had defeated into a soup that they drank to increase their prestige.

Lao-Tzu, riding in a chariot drawn by a black ox, was stopped by the Keeper of the Pass [read *gap*], Yin Hsi, who implored the sage to write a book of wisdom for him before he ventured to the mountains in the West. At the gap, he wrote the *Tao Te Ching*, one of the world's great books of wisdom, in the year 240 B.C.[1]

Here is an excerpt from Chapter Eleven:

Thirty spokes unite one hub;
It is precisely where there is nothing, that we find the usefulness of the wheel.
We fire clay and make vessels;
It is precisely where there is no substance, that we find the usefulness of clay pots.
We chisel out doors and windows;
It is precisely in these empty spaces, that we find the usefulness of the room.

Therefore, we regard having something as beneficial;
But having nothing is useful.[2]

Earlier I have written about doing nothing, citing both Dr. Henderson and Pooh Bear. On a deep level, we can contrast American action-oriented culture with the Eastern Tao principle of nonaction. This central thesis of Tao is called *wu wie*, which, translated into English, is "action in inaction." Skeptics scoff, believing that it means mere inactivity, or ridicule it as a prescription for not fighting, doing nothing, being passive. The essential meaning of an act without activity, however, is perfect action.

[1]Welch, Holmes. *Taoism: The Parting of the Way*. Boston: Beacon Press, 1966, pp. 2, 19.
[2]Hendricks, Robert G. *Te-Tao Ching*: "A New Translation of the Ma-Wang-Tue Text." New York: Ballantine Books, 1989, p. 63.

Chuang Tzu, an ancient Chinese sage, said that "action in inaction" is action not carried out independent of heaven and earth or in conflict with the dynamism of the whole, but rather in perfect harmony with the whole. It is not mere passivity. It is action that seems effortless and spontaneous performed in perfect accordance with our nature and our place in the scheme of things. It is completely free because there is no force, no violence. It is not conditioned or limited by our individual needs and desires, or our theories and ideas.

> Silence, non-action: this is the level of heaven and earth.
> This is perfect Tao. Wise men find here
> Their resting place.
> Resting, they are empty.[1]

Most patients who come to see me are not compulsive gap fillers, aggressive in assaults on silence, but they seek my attention, being ready to listen to me after I have listened to them.

I rarely interrupt my patients. There is no floor grabbing in my office because I give them the floor. Few of them are at a loss for words. I am an intense, attentive, face-to-face, silent, quiet listener. I listen for what they tell me, what they do not tell me, and what their silences tell me. Each quickly learns that I highly value dreams because they can reveal truths that consciousness does not know. Their authority comes from them, not from me. I can sit peacefully and patiently, a good indicator because almost all of my patients are impatient with their patience.

This attitude is a generic form of zazen – a Zen meditation that frees one's mind from desires, concepts, and judgment, thinking neither good nor evil and seeking tranquillity and listening within. In the true form of zazen, the meditator concentrates on breathing and seeks enlightenment, while

---

[1]Merton, Thomas. *The Way of Chuang Tzu*. Boston: Shambhala, 1991, xiii, 1, p. 30.

sitting in the cross-legged lotus position. I do not burn candles in my office, but I have a candle in case the electricity is off.

Jungian analyst, Jean-Pierre Schnetzler, writes that psychoanalysis is a cure by silence:

> To be more precise, one would have to say that fundamentally, psychoanalysis is the space in which the patient's speech is liberated by the analyst's silence. The first virtue of the analyst's silence is that it allows the patient to have the floor.[1]

Schnetzler recognizes the idea of MA and compares the analyst's silence to the Buddha nature, meditation, and the wisdom of nonduality.

The words do not count so much as listening to the intervals of silences that the words evoke. This idea is the key to understanding the Word Association Text that was the discovery of C. G. Jung. In a famous research project, he used a stopwatch to measure the intervals of silence that followed selected words to which the subject was told to relate the first thoughts that came to mind. During the test, Jung recorded the subject's pulse, galvanic skin response, blood pressure, and respiration rate. This pioneering work revealed that the telltale data was the time interval between the word and the response. Before this experiment, the word association test was based on the content of the association words. Jung's research led to the Word Association Test as a lie detector in forensic science.[2]

I have noted that the pattern of silent intervals in the flow of my patients' conversation gives a rhythm to their speech that helps explain its meaning to me – especially in dream interpretation.

---

[1]Schnetzler, Jean-Pierre. "Le Silence de la Psychanalyse à la Méditation," *Cahiers de Psychologie Jungienne*, No. 44, 1985, pp. 45-57.
[2]Jung, C. G. *Studies in Word Association*. London: Routledge & Kegan Paul, 1969 [first published in 1918].

During a symposium on dreams that I directed at the Institute for the Humanities at Salado, I told one of our major speakers that I could tell when a patient's dream story was going to end. The speaker, William Dement, was a professor of psychiatry, director of the sleep center at Stanford University, and a codiscoverer of REM sleep. He was skeptical of this novel idea, asking me to explain. I told him that I could tell by the narrative when a different stage was reached that would no longer be elaborated by images or story. It was as if the patient were telegraphing me (mental telepathy) that a denouement was about to come. Dement, a brilliant clinician and research scientist, asked me if I could send him evidence to justify my statement. I said I would, and the program continued.

Returning to my analytic practice, I secured permission from some of my patients to audiotape their dreams and our discussion. I personally transcribed and reflected on the texts of our dialogues. My explanation for knowing that the end was coming was like a literary critic discoursing on how the construction of a surreal story was concluded. While this method was convincing to me, I was aware that my interpretation depended entirely on my understanding of the patient's story conveyed in a symbolic or metaphorical story. The method I was using was too idiosyncratic and subjective to convince a healthy, logically minded skeptic.

I waited before writing Dement, listened again to the tapes, and made more recordings of patients telling me their dreams. This time, I listened to the dream tapes more skeptically and keenly, examined my new transcriptions, and had doubts. There was something missing in the transcriptions that was present in the recordings – length and patterns of silent spaces. Suddenly, I became aware that I was not making my judgment on the revealed content of the dream story, but rather on the changes in rhythm of speech as the story was being concluded. There was a different pattern of silent intervals, becoming longer and more irregular. I was identifying the coming end of a dream by the rhythm of silences.

Thinking of Jung's Word Association Test, I knew this pattern could be studied scientifically, and hoped that Bill Dement would be interested enough to follow up with some research in his famous clinical and research center. A long time passed. Knowing how involved Bill was in many activities, I cannot say that I was surprised, but I was disappointed when Bill never answered my letter with its enclosed transcriptions of dreams and tapes. It never occurred to me until I wrote this paragraph that he might never have received my answer to his question.

His silence has puzzled me all these years.

My son John and his son Jacob, my six-year-old grandson, are visiting Salado from San Francisco. This morning, Jacob and I were alone in the garden when he brought me a strange leaf, saying proudly, "never saw a leaf like this before." I looked at it very carefully and said, "Jacob, you could give it a name and it will be your discovery." He looked at me annoyed, and said, "I'm just a kid. I am sure some adult has seen one of these leaves before." By not listening carefully, I missed the real point of Jacob's bringing the leaf to me for identification and derailed in fantasyland. The moral was painfully clear: Someone else is always there before you.

My search through world literature on MA had yielded nothing about dreams until I recently discovered a book by Jill Mellick, *The Natural Artistry of Dreams*, with a section on "The Mystery of MA: Looking at What Is Missing." She refers to the empowering as the missing link between two scenes, and the room you entered without a door. Mellick discusses the function of MA in dreams as the spaces that can easily embrace paradox and present the impossible – being present in two time frames, two bodies, two genders, two places, two belief systems. Her discussion of "MA in the Open-Heart [surgery] Dream" was particularly interesting to me because of my personal ordeal with open-heart surgery.

Mellick is an artist, musician, and psychologist, deeply interested in Jungian psychology. She cites a case where she asked a patient to analyze a dream of an Eskimo ceremony by writing out the dream so that each sentence contained only one dream element, and then to experiment by removing them one by one and asking herself, "How does the feeling or mystery of the whole dream change when I remove this element?" By so doing, she better appreciated the MA behind each element.[1]

That is impressive, but not exactly like my MA leaf in dream interpretation. A number of years ago, I found myself at a troubling, depressed time. While shaving one morning, I suddenly remembered a very short dream that gave me a jolt of joy. In the dream, I was holding a strong three-ring green binder that had two pieces of paper in it. I opened the binder to the title page and saw my name on it. When I turned the page over, the second page was blank. Instantly, I said to myself, "Harry, you just turned over a new leaf!" That is a natural MA dream announcing a new beginning. A blank page, like a blank canvas, is the symbolic image that faces every writer or artist when he or she embarks on a new piece of work.

Deepak Chopra observed that the stream of consciousness as described by William James failed to notice that between every thought there is a fleeting gap of silence.

> The silent gap between thoughts, being intangible, still plays no part in modern psychology, which is oriented completely to the mind's contents or the brain's mechanisms. The gap turns out to be the central player, however, if you are interested in what lies between thoughts.[2]

Silent space without boundaries approximates the Buddhist image of the self, composed of endless points or centers

[1]Mellick, Jill. *The Natural Artistry of Dreams: Creative Ways to Bring the Wisdom of Dreams to Waking Life*. Berkeley, Calif.: Corari Press, 1996, pp. 121-126.

[2]Chopra, Deepak. *Quantum Healing: Exploring the Frontiers of Mind/Body Medicine*. New York: Bantam, 1989, p. 149.

with a circumference everywhere. In this silent space, time disappears. Einstein wrote:

> With the discovery of the relativity of simultaneity, space and time merged in a single continuum in the same way that three-dimensional space had been. Physical space was thus increased to a four-dimensional space which also included the dimension of time. The four-dimensional space of the special theory of relativity is just as rigid and absolute as Newton's space.

Einstein measured distances between events rather than objects, and involved both time and space together. Until recent times, physicists thought of space as the passive container of all events, playing no part in the physical happening itself.[1]

The origin of the universe, called The Big Bang Theory, has been described as an explosion that occurred everywhere simultaneously. Steven Weinberg, Nobel laureate in physics, says that the explosion filled all space with particles of matter rushing apart from every other particle. *All space*, in this formulation, means either all of an infinite universe or all of a finite universe that curves back on itself like the surface of a sphere.

Weinberg wrote:

> At about one-hundredth of a second, the earliest time about which we can speak with any confidence, the temperature was about a hundred thousand million degrees centigrade. This is much hotter than in the center of even the hottest star. ... As the explosion continued, the temperature diminished and at the end of three minutes things began to come together. The problem of the early universe is banished; there was no early universe.[2]

[1]Einstein, Albert in *Man and the Universe: The Philosophy of Science* edited by Saxe Commins and Robert N. Linscott. New York: Random House, 1947, pp. 471-82.

Imagining that ultimate silence preceded the Big Bang, I asked Weinberg about the noise metaphor: "Big Bang." He replied:

> As you suggest, the phrase "big bang" is indeed a metaphor, and is not intended to suggest anything about sound, only an explosive dispersal of particles of matter away from each other. There would have been some departure from perfect homogeneity in an early universe, not unlike ordinary sound waves, but these waves would have been profoundly affected by the expansion of the universe and by gravitation, eventually (we think) becoming strong enough to trigger the formation of galaxies. ... [1]

The Hubble Space Telescope, which America has orbiting space, extends our vision toward the horizon of our expanding universe seventy-two sextillion miles to see events that took place over twelve billion years ago. Up to now, that is the limit of our reach in the outer universe toward absolute silence.[2]

I imagine silent space as beyond the threshold of the cosmos, the inner margins or horizons of the ever-expanding universe, but since there is no other side or limit we cannot call it space in a conventional sense, but rather silence beyond celestial space – maybe God.

[2]Weinberg, Steven. *The First Three Minutes: A Modern View of the Origin of the Universe*. New York: Bantam, 1980.
[1]Weinberg. Personal communication (December 13, 1992).
[2]Barbree, Jay, and Martin Caidin. *A Journey Through Time: Exploring the Universe with the Hubble Space Telescope*. New York: Penguin Studio, 1995.

7

Spirit and Death:
The Ultimate Ordeal

> And what the dead had no speech for, when living,
> They can tell you, being dead: the communication
> Of the dead is tongued with fire beyond the language
> of the living.[1]

T. S. Eliot
Four Quartets

Midnight, October 14, 1997: My wife woke me – her face gaunt, terrified, and pale ... her eyes wide and tearful. She said, "Mary just called and said that Hank was killed in an automobile accident near Fulton, Missouri." We held each other, unable to talk.

Hank, or Harry A. Wilmer III, age fifty-two, was our firstborn child – a marvelous son, father, husband, and successful banker. We have three other sons and Mary, our daughter.

Hank had been driving alone to see his daughter, Arianne, a senior at Westminster College in Fulton and was several hours late. Arianne called the highway patrol. Later there was a knock at her door. It was a highway patrolman, who told her that Hank had been instantly killed when his car had been

---

[1]Eliot, T. S. "Little Gidding" in *Four Quartets*. New York: Harcourt Brace Jovanovich, 1971, (I, lines 49-51), p. 51. (On Eliot's memorial in Westminster Abbey).

thrown across the median strip, twisted, and hit on the driver's side by a speeding oncoming car. No one in that car was seriously injured. The crash occurred just ten minutes away from Arianne's house.

Following this loss, I noted a series of dreams in my diary.

Dream One

The phone rings. I am in Menlo Park, California. It is Laura Lynn, who lived across the street. She is one year younger than Hank, age ten in the dream.

"Can I talk to Hank?" she asks.

I pause – barely able to say, "Hank was killed in an automobile accident." I begin sobbing and Laura Lynn could not talk.

Dream Two

I am on a ship sailing to the North Pole. The ship lurches in a stormy sea, barely avoiding a collision with small rocky islands that suddenly appear out of the grey overcast sky above the sea. I know that our ship has sailed from the Far East, along the coast of China, around India, past Europe to Norway and on to the Arctic Ocean.

The ship reaches the North Pole, and drops anchor at a snow and glacier-covered island about one mile long. In front of us is a small village where Eskimos live year-round.

I tell the people on the ship that we can go ashore and learn from the Eskimo about survival in the Arctic. A sailor calls me to the ship telephone where I have a call from the United States. A voice expresses sadness and condolence about Hank's death.

Commentary: Since Hank's death I have been depressed, exhausted with grief, and barely able to speak on the phone about him. My sleep was extremely restless the night of the dream. The story is going to the top of the world to learn how to survive in extreme cold.

I have observed that the North Pole is often associated with death in dreams. In reality, there are no rocky islands near the North Pole, and no Eskimo living anywhere near. It is uninhabitable land where nothing grows.

The image is a mythical dream island with people who survive extreme cold. Beyond the Arctic Circle, the Arctic Ocean around the North Pole is covered by a solid, but not very thick ice pack. The pole cannot be reached by a surface ship, only by nuclear submarine or airplane.

The dream, I think, holds out hope of learning to endure the harsh times of mourning and grief – learning from native human beings who live and die on the ice.

Why did I dream of the North Pole? From July 25 to August 1, 1997, Jane and I were on an Arctic exploration cruise around the archipelago of Svalbard or Spitsbergen, at 74°81' north latitude, six hundred miles from the North Pole. On our return home, Hank was extremely interested in our journey and wanted to go to the Arctic.

Dream Three

I am in the Swiss Alps walking in a colorful deep valley surrounded by steep snow-covered mountains. The scene changes and I am rowing an ordinary rowboat on a large, very deep lake surrounded by dark mountains rising almost straight up from the water's edge. In the dream, it reminded me of the Lake of Lucerne.

In contrast to the colorful warm valley, the lake scene is cold, grey, and bleak, almost like a mosaic of grey and white.

I now realize that Hank is in the boat with me. We are silent. The rowboat moves along smoothly until the wind starts blowing very hard from my back – sweeping the boat far out into the silver-grey lake. The storm blows waves as high as ten feet. I know that I must find the strength to turn the boat around, and row as hard as I can, to get back to the shore.

When I begin rowing, I know that we will make it. At this point, the classical Swiss scene becomes the American West. I extol the grandeur of this awesome American scene to a man in the boat who has taken the place of Hank. I tell him how surprisingly easy it was to row back to shore against the waves.

Commentary: This dream is a journey of grief in a storm on a large lake where Hank and I are being swept far out. Forcing myself to use all the energy I can muster, I turn the rowboat around. Then everything calms down and even the monstrous waves are no longer obstacles. Hank's silent presence suggests the metaphor that I am at sea with him. Hank's silent spirit is replaced by an unidentified male companion, probably one of my other sons.

I have spent so much time in Switzerland over the past twenty-six years that it seems like a second home to me. I know that the further west you sail on the Lake of Lucerne, the steep mountains seem to close in, and during a storm, I have felt a sense of great danger.

The change from Switzerland to the American frontier is reminiscent of the story of the Lewis and Clark Expedition that I had just seen on television. Earlier in this book, I noted that the American Western expansion began by passing through the Cumberland Mountain Gap – valley – to reach the Missouri [sic] River on which the Lewis and Clark Expedition intended to row and sail large canoe-like boats through the Rocky Mountains to the Pacific Ocean.

Perhaps this dream is like another edition of the reports from my unconscious on how I am coping with the terrible loss of my wonderful son at the prime of his life. The message is positive. The dream is comforting, because it tells me that I have the strength to turn things around, and make it back to *terra firma*. This is the journey that I was destined to take with Hank.

The scene could be associated with the ancient myth that a dead person must be ferried by Charon across the River Styx to Elysium.

The silence of shock is being aghast at a sudden overwhelming encounter with a horrible event that stuns one by the feeling of total helplessness and powerlessness to intervene for others. Earlier, when I reported posttraumatic stress disorder and the classical catastrophe war nightmare, the critical traumatic event was always about the death or mutilation of another close soldier, not the veteran's own death. This situation is known as survivor guilt, which – real or imagined – stirs the fires of the unconscious. I have written about working with their dreams, which I called *The Healing Nightmare*.[1] Now I will tell you how I worked with my own dreams to help myself understand, and find some glimmer of meaning to counter the general feeling of the meaninglessness of the tragedy – or the hand of fate.

Two days before Hank's tragic death, on October 24, he wrote to his sister, Mary, a letter full of optimism and hope for the future. He ended it by saying, "I am off to see Arianne on Friday and Saturday. It should be fun. She, like her sister, is growing into a wonderful young adult." Mary wrote Hank a letter of reply on October 27, which she read at his funeral:

Dear Hank,

Thanks for your wonderful letter, and for your insights about turn-arounds. The whole family, your friends, and the people who have worked with you, now need to learn from your wisdom and enthusiasm about turning around tough situations. You see, we are all in a tailspin, reeling from the thought of not having you with us. We will miss your contagious, charming boyish smile, and that sparkle in your eyes. We will miss your great sense of humor and severely bad puns. We will miss you as a brother, a nephew, a husband, a father, an uncle, a boss, a co-worker and to all

---

[1]Wilmer, Harry A. *The Healing Nightmare* (a book in process).

a dear friend. The most amazing thing is that in our family, full of different opinions, we all agreed that we were 100% blessed to have had you in our lives. We just didn't think, didn't even dare think, you would leave us so early.

All my love,
Mary

Hank's wife Lynn wrote of Hank's spirit:

He loved people so much and he was never judgmental. He employed his intelligence and generosity of spirit each and every day. He awoke each day with enthusiasm and determination. He was not a person who prayed to God or meditated. He lived his life with goodness and integrity. His eyes had a sparkling light in them shining out at the world around him. I find it impossible to put a definitive label on what he was: I can only say that he was. His life and actions speak of the pureness of his spirit. I miss him so much it is hard to bear. Our daughters can't imagine never speaking with him again or never again enjoying a big hug from his strong body. He was a wonderful man, and all who knew him bear witness to the blessing of Hank's life.

My Diary entry, January 26, 1998: "In this dark time of grief, Hank's image seems everywhere, clear, strong with a warm smile of recognition. I marvel at what I see and remember. There is a radiance, and my soul's eye accommodates to the darkness that struck with his sudden violent death. Light illuminates the shadow of the valley of death. Hank's presence, even now, comforts and holds my sadness and tears. In death the invisible filial bond is as strong as in life. If this is a gleam of heaven, then we are with Hank."

Synchronicity

> *Synchronicity:* the simultaneous occurrence of events which appear meaningfully related but there is no discoverable causal connection.[1]

In contrast to the synchronous, simple simultaneous occurrence of two events, synchronicity is the simultaneous occurrence of two meaningfully but not causally connected events in which an inner psychic subjective state or event parallels an outer event in the objective world. Not only is the cause unknown, but the cause is not even thinkable.[2]

Seemingly coincidental events have occurred related to silence and Hank's death that represent synchronicity.

For example, in the last chapter on MA, I have acknowledged the help of the Japanese psychiatrist, Osamu Kuramitsu, who came from Japan to spend a month with me studying Jungian psychology. During his stay, he attended my seminar and lecture at the Institute for the Humanities on "The Quest for Silence" on April 6, 1996. This was the first and only major presentation I have given at the institute, which I had founded in 1980. I spoke about my book on silence. It so happened that my son Hank had come from Chicago to attend my lecture.

I introduced Osamu to Hank before the lecture and introduced Osamu to the audience. He arose, told them that he had been the Japanese translator of my book, *Practical Jung*, which I have just quoted on the subject of synchronicity. Then, smiling broadly, he announced that he was my new son – to the surprise and pleasure of both myself and the audience.

After Osamu returned to Japan, he wrote me occasionally, and I would promptly reply. Then I received a letter shortly after Hank's death, and was unable to get to any mail for over

---

[1]*The New Shorter Oxford English Dictionary*, Vol. 2. Oxford, England: Clarendon Press, 1993, p. 3188.

[2]Wilmer, Harry A. *Practical Jung: Nuts and Bolts of Jungian Psychotherapy.* Wilmette, IL.: Chiron Publications, 1987, pp. 170-72.

a month, and it was even longer before I could bring myself to write Osamu and explain my long silence. I also told him that Jane and I had endowed a Harry Wilmer III Memorial Lectureship at the Institute, and the first speaker this June would be Jeffrey Burton Russell on his new book, *A History of Heaven: The Singing Silence.*[1]

It was a long time before I heard from Osamu, who liked to be called "Sam." Then, on April 4, 1998, I received a letter enclosed in a card with a painting of Vincent Van Gogh entitled "First Steps," from the Metropolitan Museum of Art. The picture showed a child held up by the mother, with one arm reaching out to the father, who was crouching with wide open arms by a wheelbarrow in a vegetable garden.

The letter from Osamu read:

Dear Dr. Wilmer:
About a month has passed since I got your sad letter. I am sorry I could not write you until now. I could not find proper words that express my feelings though I have been thinking of you often.
Just after I read your letter I got in my car and started the engine, when this song by Eric Clapton came to my ears from the first note. I was so moved that I wanted to send this tape to you soon, but it took me some time to carry it out anyway. [Clapton sang the song "Tears in Heaven" about the accidental death of his son.]
Do you know the song "Imagine" by John Lennon, in which he sings, "Imagine there's no heaven"? When I was young I thought it would be fine, but now I imagine there are multiple heavens. I dream that you might meet your son Hank in heaven and even now in your deep layer of your psyche. As heaven is the land where the rules of time and space of our daily world might be overcome, I hope souls who really want to meet must have some communi-

[1]Russell, Jeffrey Burton. *A History of Heaven: The Singing Silence.* Princeton, N.J.: Princeton University Press, 1997.

cation. I can even imagine Hank consoles you there somehow.

My wise old man, Dr. Wilmer, I feel our lives are woven in mysterious ways. ... I feel our spirit will succeed in another generation. I know I'm not like your real true son, Hank. I have been influenced by you. Even though relatively short period of meeting, my life has been changed by you. I hope someday we meet again in this world or in our dreams or in heaven.

With love and deep respects,
O. Kuramitsu
Sam

My Death

When I think of my death, it comes to me in a poem I wrote for Jane:

The Dying Grieve for Those They Love

When your time comes,
Time becomes dead time.
You are silently passing away,
Then you are gone
To rest in silence.

You are not gone for good,
Nor gone for bad,
But gone for sure.

I survive, though dying
I cry and grieve,
Silently dying alone,
Seeing you.

We speak of joining,
Though we shall not know whether

It was you who died, and I who mourned,
Or I who died and you who grieved.

We shall be buried side by side
In death's sweet embrace.
Weep no more.
In silence, sing to me.

The Unfillable Gaps: Death and the Black Hole

When Americans are faced with gaps they cannot fill, they deny them. Death is passing away and being gone. Doctors perform heroic deeds in fighting death as an enemy, with a zeal that often has horrible effects. The dead soldiers from the Korean and Vietnam Wars were forgotten in a national amnesia. The lost wars and dead are a dark gap we cannot fill. For decades, they fall into the category of forgotten meaninglessness.

Ernest Becker, professor of political science, sociology, and anthropology at Simon Fraser University in Canada, won the Pulitzer Prize in 1974 for his book, *The Denial of Death*, published one year before he died. Becker cites Freud's great contribution, that each of us repeats the tragedy of the mythical Greek, Narcissus: We are hopelessly absorbed with ourselves.

> If we care about anyone it is usually ourselves first. As Aristotle somewhere put it: luck is when the guy next to you gets hit with the arrow. ... The great perplexity of our time, the churning of our age, is that youth has sensed – for better or worse – a great social-historical truth: that just as there are useless self-sacrifices in unjust wars, so too, there is an ignoble heroics of whole societies.

Becker reminds us that heroism is first and foremost a reflex terror of death, and that the hero in ancient times was the man who could go into the spirit world, the world of the dead, and return alive. Becker concludes that science is a credo that has attempted to absorb into itself, and to deny the fear of life and death.

> Modern man is drinking and drugging himself out of awareness, or he spends his time shopping, which is the same thing. As awareness calls for types of heroic dedication that his culture no longer provides for him, society contrives to help him forget. Or alternately, he buries himself in psychology in the belief that awareness all by itself will be some kind of magical cure for his problems. But psychology was born with the breakdown of shared social heroisms; it can only be gone beyond with the creation of new heroisms that are basically matters of belief and will, dedication to a vision.[1]

The Black Hole and the Death of the Sun

A black hole is a region in space from which matter and radiation cannot escape due to the intense gravitational pull, thought to have been created by the collapse of massive stars. Matter is drawn into the black hole and at the edge of the black hole, emitting radiation at the horizon of the black hole into which matter collapses. Our sun is expected to be consumed by its core and will exist as a red giant for a few thousand million years.

> Afterwards in its last "visible" incarnation – as a slowly cooling dying ember of a white dwarf – the sun will persist for a few more thousands of millions of years, finally obtaining total obscurity as an invisible black dwarf.[2]

[1]Becker, Ernest. *The Denial of Death*. New York: Free Press, 1973, pp. 2, 7, 11, 12, 284.
[2]Penrose, Roger. *The Emperor's New Mind: Concerning Computers, Minds, and Laws of Physics.* New York: Oxford University Press, 1989, p. 330.

Avoiding Another Dark Age

> The worst is death, and death will have his day.
> – Shakespeare, *Richard II*

Ugly death is the hallmark of cruelty, genocide, massacre, and the slaughterhouse of war. People starve and execute others, maraud in death squads, hack and decapitate their fellow humans. People are tortured to death, or so destroyed by torture as to become the living dead. Death and dying, like silence, have their grotesque forms.

People die with almost unbearable pain and angst, even under the care of physicians – who prescribe inadequate medication, or in lands where there are no physicians or medication. Hospitals prolong life and suffering so that death does not come as a friend but as an unconquerable enemy to be fought to a prolonged bitter end. Doctors use what they call "heroic measures" to fight off death. Impersonal forces get in the act: Doctors become providers, patients become customers or consumers, insurance companies and managed-care voices over telephones dictate treatment to physicians to guarantee cost-effective, very profitable health care. Lawyers, judges, moralists, and legalistic ethicists sicken the dying process. When our bodies are encased in hospitals, we lose charge of our bodies, minds, and souls. We regress in paternalistic and maternalistic systems.

The humanistic realm has lost to the technologic and scientific world when the only real hope is their meeting. This state of affairs reflects our national cultural changes toward polarization, litigious obsession, distrust, meanness, loss of civility, and manners. Compassion has been reduced to a buzzword and lost its spiritual meaning. We talk of compassion fatigue, political compassion, and wonder if we can afford compassion.

Compassion is a state that does not fatigue, has no ulterior aims, and cannot be meted out on an accounting basis. The human spirit has been given the silent treatment for its own good. We stand witness to a growing coldness of hearts, shriveling mercy, and uprooted *caritas*. Nevertheless, there are always strong forces of caring in unlikely places and dedicated individuals nurturing and taking care of the human spirit. To these we must turn to avoid another Dark Age.

We must understand Nature and not be slaves to science and statistics. Anthropologist, Steven Feld, has made a career of listening to and recording the sounds of birds in the jungles of Kaluli, New Guinea. For years, he collected and organized experimental field information on bird taxonomy and identification in the forests and villages trying to specify the zoological content of closely related Kaluli taxa. Jubi was his native helper. After coming to an impasse after months of field work, Feld realized that the weakness of his work was due to his personal conception of how culture interprets Nature. It was Jubi who made the professor understand.

Feld writes:

With characteristic patience, Jubi was imitating calls, behavior, and nesting. Suddenly something snapped: I asked a question and Jubi blurted back, "Listen – to you they are birds, to me they are voices in the forest." I was startled because it was so direct (Kaluli tend to be very direct, confrontational in face-to-face interaction) but [also] because it so thoroughly expressed the necessity of approaching natural history as a part of a cultural system. Jubi's comment was symptomatic of my naive acceptance of the proclamation that ethnoscience was a way to meet the natives on their own terms … "To you they are birds" meant that I was forcing a method of knowledge construction – isolation and education – onto the domain of experience that Kaluli do not isolate and reduce. "To me they are voices in the forest" meant that there are many ways to think about birds, depending on the context in which knowledge is activated and social needs are served. Birds are voices because Kaluli recognize and acknowledge primarily through sound, and because they are the spirit reflections [*ane mama*] of deceased men and women. Bird sounds simultaneously have an outside – from which Kaluli attribute a bird's identification, and an inside – from which they interpret the underlying meaning as a spirit communication.[1]

---

[1]Feld, Steven. *Sound and Sentiment: Birds, Weeping, Poetics, and Song in Kaluli Expression.* Philadelphia: University of Pennsylvania Press, 1982, pp. 44-46.

8

Patience

In your patience possess ye your souls.
Luke 21:19

A porcelain figure of a little boy looking up to the sky and holding a flower pot in his arm rests near the consultation chair in my office. It has been there since 1957 and fascinates me with its elegance – innocent and looking up hopefully.

The figure is a Danish Bing and Grundall statuette. Every time I gaze at it, I think it is called "Who's Listening?" As soon as I say that, however, I correct myself to remember that the artist gave it the name "Who's Calling?"

There is a big difference between "Who's listening?" and "Who's calling?" The former leaves open the question that maybe no one is there, or if there is, that person is unknown. The latter suggests an unrecognized voice from an unseen person reaching out to the little boy, speaking to him. It is a silent other and a wondering, listening, looking child. It calls my attention to the work of an analyst.

Let us examine silence through the arts.

Literature: I wrote to author Sir Laurens van der Post in London on November 25, 1995, inviting him to fly to Salado to speak on the subject of silence the next fall. He eagerly accepted my invitation. Laurens died quite suddenly at the age of ninety, however, a few weeks before he was to fly to America. He had concluded his letter of acceptance with these words:

The longer one lives the more eloquent and important the silence to which you refer becomes. What we ultimately think of as the greatest of all silences is but a marshaling yard of creation of the – as yet – unuttered voices of the future.[1]

We have no alternative but to wait patiently for those voices to be spoken – until the future, in due time, becomes the present.

Art: The silent, empty spaces are the mystery we do not know, but which give meaning rhythm, and aesthetic value to the objects in which they exist. I have referred to the painter Claude Monet, and now turn to the stone and bronze sculptures of Henry Moore.

Moore created large sculptures with gaps of empty spaces within and between the mass. Walking around his sculptures, you see these empty spaces change. The shapes play upon each other because Moore was sculpturing not only the stone or bronze but also the spaces between, which created an unusual liveliness.

Dr. Michael Brown, molecular geneticist at Southwestern University Medical School in Dallas, won the Nobel Prize for physiology or medicine in 1958 for his work with Joseph Goldstein on cholesterol metabolism and the discovery of low-density or LDL receptors. In Brown's lecture at the Salado institute, he spoke of Henry Moore's bronze sculptures in this way:

> A doctor, a physician, has to concentrate on the bronze, the hard masses of facts that are there, whereas the scientist has to concentrate on the open spaces between the bronze. The scientist has to know where the gaps are in our knowledge, where the frontier is …, and has to almost forget about what is known. If you are so bound by what's known, you are not going to have the novel thought – that ingenious novel idea of something fresh.[2]

[1]van der Post, Sir Laurens. Personal communication.

Music: Roger Penrose, Rouse professor of mathematics at Oxford University, shared the 1988 Wolf Prize with Stephen Hawking for their joint contribution to the understanding of the universe. Penrose in his book, *The Emperor's New Mind*, wrote on the strange role of time in conscious perception:

> Listen to the quadruple fugue in the final part of J. S. Bach's Art of Fugue. No one with a feeling for Bach's music can help being moved as the music stops after ten minutes of performance, just after the third theme enters. The composition as a whole still seems to be "there," but now it has faded from us in an instant. Bach died before he was able to complete the work, and his musical score simply stops at that point, with no written indication as to how he intended it to continue. Yet it starts with such an assurance and total mastery that one cannot imagine that Bach did not hold the entire composition in his mind at the time.[1]

The Great MAW

While I write a lot, there have been long periods of time when I do not write anything I would call creative. Writer's block may last for short periods or for decades. By adding the letter "W" onto "MA," we have the gaping space I call the Great MAW. MAW is defined in the dictionary as "the cavity of the stomach or abdomen, the belly, the womb, the throat or jaws of a voracious animal or fish."

I had been writing and rewriting this book for several years, when one night, as I was walking up the hill to my greenhouse, I felt a sudden stabbing pain in my right thigh. I stopped, so weak and dizzy that I thought I would faint. I let myself fall to the ground before I passed out. This occurred about ten yards from our house, where I could see Jane in the

[2]Brown, Michael. Address at the Institute for the Humanities at Salado (Salado, Texas), November 3, 1996.
[1]Penrose. *The Emperor's New Mind*, p. 445.

kitchen light but was unable to call her. When I fell, I let my briefcase drop. I tried to retrieve my cellular phone from the briefcase to call Jane, but it was just out of reach. My voice was so weak I was reminded of dreams when one tries to call out but no sounds emerge, or when one tries to move but moves in slow motion or is paralyzed.

When I was finally able to crawl back home, I went directly to bed followed by an anxious Jane. When my neighbor doctor from across the street came to see me, he told me that I had a severe hemorrhage in my anterior groin and thigh muscles. He urged me to let him call an ambulance to take me to the emergency room.

It did not seem to me that there was anything they could do in the hospital except observe me and that could be done better at home.

I would not go to the hospital. Jane brought me cold compresses, and I endured the pain with medication.

Within a few days, my entire right leg was black and blue from toes to thigh, tightly swollen, and very tender. I went to the doctor's office where blood tests showed anemia requiring iron medication. I remained in bed at home, my leg elevated with cold compresses day and night.

For several years, I had been writing this book in longhand on yellow paper pads at every available moment. I was also very busy with other commitments, running the Salado Institute, seeing students and patients, and generally trying to do too much without taking the necessary reflective time to write and patiently weave my book.

After three weeks in bed, I could sit up, but had no desire to resume writing. The drive was dead. What had happened was like a bolt out of the blue striking me. I felt indifference, but no depression.

The doctor and I concluded that I had a sharp muscle cramp in my leg the morning of my lightning bolt, and I had massaged it to no effect. Then I hit the cramped muscle with my fist several times. Rather than breaking up the cramp, I had started a hemorrhage that bled slowly all day and into the early evening which made me so anemic that I collapsed.

When I did get out of bed, I regressed into the noisy world of watching television news, stories, and drama, and ugly political noise and meanness – the exact toxic noise that I had been attacking. During all this time Jane was worried, devoted, taking care of me, cheerful but frightened, watching me in disbelief as I got hooked on the tube.

I asked myself, "Why the long silence in writing?" A fear crossed my mind that I would die before I finished my book. Then suddenly, on the twenty-sixth day, my energy and creative spirit returned like a tidal wave. Writing began to flow as before the blow. I decided to move into the present time and ordered a Macintosh computer with a laser printer and began the awkward process of learning how to use the wonder machine at age seventy-nine. After mastering the word processor, the manuscript began slowly to unfold before my eyes on my large monitor.

It was only natural that, being an analyst, I would probe my psyche to see if I could understand how, why, and when this writer's block had happened. I concluded that the writing silence that had struck me was the hand of fate: a warning to stop trying to do so many things, and stop trying to do too much for other people. The time had come to realize that charity (*caritas*: love) begins at home. It was important to quit being an American extravert and become my natural introverted self – a swift lesson in human vulnerability and morbidity. This epiphany was an awakening to pursue the art of patience and equanimity that I preached, to learn the lesson of my book the hard way.

It reminds me of the Texas story about a rancher whose mule wouldn't budge, so he hit him over the head with a two by four. The donkey fell unconscious to the ground. His ranch hand asked him why he had done that. He replied, "I had to get his attention first."

Author, Tillie Olsen, published a book entitled *Silences*, which examined the authors who had suffered years of silence. Olsen had experienced a writer's block in the twenty years she bore and reared her children and worked on a job as well. She says that the classic example of this condition relates to death, or the life-and-death tragedy, the words of the last book being metaphorically the author's dying words. Although there are exceptions, in general, being unable to write anything that is felt to have merit is anguish. She suggests that it is as if life's meaning took an endless holiday. While she focused mainly on twentieth century women, she also discussed Thomas Hardy, Gerald Manley Hopkins, Arthur Rimbaud, and Herman Melville.[1]

Herman Melville's story, *Billy Budd,* was written after thirty years of writer's silence following the publication of *Moby Dick*, which critics declared incomprehensible and the public ignored. Melville lost heart, quit writing, and worked as a customs inspector. *Billy Budd* was not published until thirty-three years after his death. The story is about a Christlike handsome young sailor who was tongue-tied, unable to speak to defend his life when falsely accused of mutiny. It is a story of innocence and good against evil in time of war. Billy was hung from the yardarm of the warship HMS *Indomitable*.[2]

Patience and Waiting

The *Oxford English Dictionary* defines *patience* as suffering or enduring of pain, trouble or evil with calmness and composure; as forbearance, long suffering, longanimity under provocation of any kind; as the calm abiding of the issue of time and processes; as the quiet and self-possessed waiting for something; and as the quality of expecting something for a long time without rage or discontent.[3]

---

[1]Olsen, Tillie. *Silences*. New York: Dell, 1978.
[2]Melville, Herman. *Billy Budd*. New York: New American Library, 1961.
[3]*The Compact Edition of the Oxford English Dictionary*, Vol. II. Oxford, England: Oxford University Press, 1979, p. 555.

In Samuel Beckett's play, *Waiting for Godot*, two tramps wait impatiently for Godot, who remains a mysterious entity. They are estranged from a state of grace that is hoped for but never realized. Often considering suicide, they are caught in a calm of inactivity between hope and despair in their longing for salvation, which is linked somehow with Godot. When the play ends, the two are still waiting for the promised appearance of Godot. The most common view sees Godot as God, with the "-ot" as a diminutive suffix.[1]

I want to relate the highlights of a psychotherapy hour with a schizophrenic patient I saw in my office once a week. The name I will give him is Francis. He functioned adequately or at least marginally at work, despite hallucinations and delusions which he managed to hide. He worked in a hospital and clinic. Although he moved and talked slowly he was hyper-alert and not negligent at work.

To maintain his control, Francis assumed a calm patient *persona* which disguised his madness. Most psychiatrists do not employ psychotherapy with psychotic patients, but instead rely solely on medication and follow-up observations. It had always been my reasoning that a "patient" calm human relationship between patient and doctor was as important as any medication. I did prescribe antipsychotic medication.

Francis is a name I have probably chosen because of my association with Saint Francis' personal tragedy, madness, and redeeming spiritual work. The patient came to see me because I was a Jungian analyst and he thought I would understand his life predicament. Francis was regular in keeping his appointments, and he would recount his weekly experiences with a bland unemotional affect. For the most part, we sat together in long periods of silent communication. There was little talk, and few interpretations. He told me his dreams.

One day he came in speaking more softly and slowly than usual. Cupping one hand over my ear, I still could not hear his

[1] Magill, Frank N. *Masterpieces of World Literature*. New York: Harper & Row, 1989, pp. 929-30.

words clearly. I explained my problem and excused myself while I walked into the next room where I had left my new hearing aids. I did not interpret my forgetting or ask him for his thoughts, but just took it as a fact in reality.

When I returned with my hearing aids in my ears, I was bewildered because I heard him even less clearly. Thinking that the batteries were dead, I put two new batteries in their place. That was it! There was a very long silence that I broke by asking him, "May I tell you a joke?"

Francis smiled and said, "Sure."

I continued, "You know, even with my new hearing aids and new batteries I don't hear anything."

He responded, "That's my life."

We talked a little and then I observed, "I notice that you don't look at me much today. You look out the window most of the time."

Francis, blushing and embarrassed, turned to look me in the eyes and said, "I wasn't aware. [Pause] Maybe that has something to do with my wanting to give up my work and stop therapy and become a beach bum."

A very long silence followed. It occurred to me that my frustration and forgetting my new hearing aids might have registered in his sensitive mind as my not being interested in his plight. His next comment seemed to suggest that.

"I haven't heard from my father or my mother for a year," he said.

The rest of the hour went on with a slow conversation about the value of work. At the end of our time, I renewed our association by saying, "I'll see you same time next week."

Francis: "Sure."

My notes for the next week's hour state: Mostly I was listening. It was as if we were sitting next to each other on a park bench, now and then feeding the birds, occasionally passing the time of day talking about something, and now and then we laughed. Same time, same bench, next Tuesday. Recycle.

The I-Thou/I-It Cycle

Linear time goes from one point to another, but time cycles around the clock, day and night, year to year. Midnight is the end of one day and the instant of another, *ad infinitum*.

We all find ourselves going in circles, when we want to straighten ourselves out. The race has a starting and an ending and we bet on the winners. The pole vault is a one-direction hop, but the pendulum swings back and forth and in a circle, showing us how the earth rotates on its axis. Sooner or later everything runs into its opposite – hero becomes shadow or trickster becomes redeemer, and on and on.

Heraclitus, in 500 B.C. Greece, saw the universe as a conflict of opposites, and gave us the law of Enantiodromia – that is, running contrariwise so that eventually everything becomes its opposite. Enantiodromia is a balance like the yin/yang or Tai Chi principle. Jung expressed this idea in a practical psychology:

> It is a bewildering thing in human life that the thing that is the greatest fear is the source of the greatest wisdom. One's greatest foolishness is one's biggest stepping stone. No one can be a wise man without being a terrible fool. Through Eros one learns the truth, through sins we learn virtue.[1]

When humans meet humans, Martin Buber postulated the idea of I-Thou (Thou being the person in the preferable form of subjective relationship) and I-It (referring to an object relationship). Usually when people hear Buber's formulation, they believe that achieving I-Thou is an end goal, but Buber's concept is that every I-Thou eventually turns into its opposite, I-It, and the cycle goes on.

[1]Jung, C. G. "Dream Analysis" (seminars, mimeograph of original), 1929, p. 26.

If Thou Art You

When the noisy "It" becomes the silent "Thou,"
The silent "Thou" is all ready to be transformed
Back into a noisy "It."
If Thou art you, who art It?
We need more transistors to work that out.
Will both Trans-sisters please expatiate?

When silence breaks out
The great polar bear walks the frozen tundra
Stalking ye.
If he eats ye, Thou becomest It.
Don't ever forget the food chain.
It has been cycling since the beginning of life.
But how does humanity come into relationship?[1]

Martin Buber cites two primary (coupled) words that signify relations: *I-Thou*, which can be spoken with the whole being, and *I-It*, which can never be spoken with the whole being (and the words *He* or *She* can replace *It*). The primary word *I-Thou* establishes the world of relations.

Buber writes:

But this is the exalted melancholy of our fate, that every Thou in our world must become an It. It does not matter how exclusively present the Thou was in direct relation. As soon as the relation has been worked out, or has been permeated with a means, the Thou becomes an object among objects. ... Every Thou in the world is by its nature fated to become a thing, is able to appear an I as its Thou. ... I-Thou is the reciprocal relation of person to person, while I-It is a relation of person to thing, subject to object. God is the eternal Thou.[2]

[1] Wilmer, Harry.
[2] Buber, Martin. *I and Thou*, 2nd ed. New York: Charles Scribner's Sons, 1958.

There is an undivided silent unity in the wordless depth in which we cannot impose the absolutized I and Thou with dialogue.[1]

Meditation, Contemplation, and No-Mind

Meditation is usually a form of disciplined silence for a time when individuals deliberately program their breathing and either focus on an object to empty their minds of ordinary preoccupations and trivia, or actively meditate on a thought or idea seeking insight or enlightenment. Meditation is a method of escaping our ordinary obsessive thinking and preoccupations, and attaining a sense of peace, quiet, and contentment. Meditators usually have a private secluded place of solitude.

It is usually not recognized that some individuals have spontaneous moments of meditation in the course of their ordinary speech. For example, Joseph Brodsky observed:

His speech consisted, on the whole, of pauses that always made you feel uneasy, since we ordinarily interpret silence to mean a person's mind is busy working. And his, in fact, was nothing but pure silence.[2]

Some people appear to disappear into a sort of fugue, and their minds empty. It seems to observers that they are not there, as if having left their bodies. I often ask my patients when they stop talking and go into blank moments, "Where did you go?" One of the most striking examples of this variety of absentmindedness has been observed in the Eskimo, or Inuit.

[1]Herberg, Will. *The Writings of Martin Buber*. New York: Meridian Books, 1956.
[2]Brodsky, Joseph. *A Part of Speech*. New York: Strauss and Giroux, 1986, p. 11.

Arctic anthropologist, Edmund Carpenter, describes:

> ... Eskimo sitting silently in an igloo waiting for clear weather. Early ethnologists suggested that such Eskimo were in self-induced trances. One Freudian said they were suppressing anxiety. In each case it was assumed that an inner dialogue had been displaced. But "conversation with self," far from being universal, is largely a product of literacy. It belongs to the literate man whose mind is a never ending clock which his will cannot stop, sleep suspends only briefly, madness and liquor cannot still, and death alone silences.
>
> I don't believe that the silent Eskimo with impassive face is thinking anything. He is just not "with it" where "it" means all senses, action, especially hunting which he loves above all else. When an Eskimo thinks, he moves, and when he speaks, he moves.[1]

A Word on the Temper of Our Times

I hate jargon, but it is the dialect of so many people that I will speak it to communicate with them. Whenever I use the words *me* and *them*, I know I am referring to my own unconscious shadow. Jargon à la Jung. I come to the conclusion that America, the gap-filling society, is inhabited with a breed of narcissistic moralists. In this place, we live the myth of Narcissus. In our postliterate, electronic society, *them* who are on top condescend to cast moralistic, righteous, and opinionated opinions of *us*, their captive audience. They are pleased with themselves as refreshingly rude. We need a new breed of mantra creating spirits. May our grossly impatient moralists fall into the well at the Spa of Deep Silence where Healthy Narcissism patiently flourishes.

---

[1]Carpenter, Edmund. *They Became What They Beheld.* New York: Ballantine, 1970.

Meditation and Yoga

The mantra, in Buddhism and Hinduism, is a repeated holy name, word, refrain, or sentence used as a prayer or incantation for inward meditation. A mantra is a word of power. For example, in Yoga, the sacred word AUM helps one meditate on the four states of consciousness. A is waking life, U is dream, and M is deep sleep. The fourth is the state of *Samadhi*, or pure consciousness expressing our divinity and unity with the whole creation.

Ernest Wood, in his book *Yoga*, concludes that hearing of the sound becomes an inward attention to still the outward curiosity of the senses, and the tendency of the mind to drift. "When the practice becomes successful on account of regularity, the last of all sounds is heard – that from the heart, called the unstruck (*anāhata*) sound in contrast to the previous sounds, which have died away and been replaced by this one. The sounds are not in themselves of value. ... Then, when the mind itself disappears (one is no longer thinking of it), there is the veritable supreme place (or rather, standing place) of Vishnu, the very heart and sustaining principle of conscious life.

"When Yoga meditation turns to contemplation, thinking is exhausted and illumination or insight comes. By that, the great sounds of our troubles: ignorance, egotism, aversions, and possessiveness are silenced."[1]

Yoga meditation begins with concentration on a single point, an object like the space between the eyebrows, the tip of the nose, something luminous, or a thought (a metaphysical truth), or God.

The way to samadhi in Yoga is akin to the path to nirvana in Buddhism and the possession of miraculous powers. The Buddhist monk must die in his earthly life to be reborn in an unconditioned state. Nirvana, which literally means "to blow

[1]Wood, Ernest. *Yoga*. New York: Penguin Books, 1968, pp. 136-190.

off" or "extinction" is the state of perfect tranquillity, where there is no object, no self, no ego, and no mind.

Yoga technique is described in the Indian *Bhagavad-Gita* in which the Yogi's soul is continually devoted to meditation, with mind under control, to reach the final boundary of nirvana.[1]

These mystical ways are remote from American noisy consciousness, which is probably why they have fascinated many thoughtful people. Unfortunately, Americans want what they want fast, and with rare exceptions, are unwilling or unable to devote the years, or lifetime, to achieve the rewards of Yoga's mystical devotion. Characteristically we opt out for short versions – classes, lectures, workshops, and pop-Yoga personalities – to learn about Yoga. Some people even travel to India to find their guru. Jungian analysts study such Eastern philosophies as manifestations of the collective unconscious.

Meditators focus on a point, object, or mantra to keep the foreground in mind while the background floats away. The purpose is to free oneself from attachments and distraction and to seek wholeness in silence. After meditation, the next step is contemplation, usually in some religious frame.

The Monastery

The monk seeks both solitude and silence, and the silent response to silence in relationship. Reflecting on his monastic experience as a Cistercian or Trappist monk, Thomas Merton, who took the vow of silence, explained:

> The solitary life, being silent, clears away the smoke-screen of words that man has laid down between his mind and things. ... Words stand between silence and silence:

[1]Eliade, Mircea. *Yoga: Immortality and Freedom*, 2nd ed. Princeton, N.J.: Princeton University Press, 1973, pp. 47, 159, 177.

between the silence of things and the silence of our own being, between the silence of the world and the silence of God. When we have really met and known the world of silence, words do not separate us from the world nor from other men, nor from God, nor from ourselves because we no longer trust entirely in language to contain reality.

Merton wrote that silence is his salvation.

My knowledge of myself in silence (not my reflection on myself, but by penetrating to the mystery of my true self which is beyond words and concepts because it is utterly particular) opens out into the silence and the subjectivity of God's own self. ... As soon as he speaks my name, my silence is the silence of infinite life, and I know I am because my heart has opened to my Father in the echo of the eternal years. My life is a listening. His is a speaking. My salvation is to hear and respond. For this, my life must be silent. Hence my silence is my salvation.[1]

Many Americans seek to spend time in monastic retreats. The psyche (meaning soul) hungers to be reunited with silent bliss as it forever yearns to return to the warm security symbolic of the womb. The solitude and silence that the monastery embodies are not the place, but a state of mind. A person may also find solitude and silence in a forest, the desert, or mountains. Most individuals do not find the frame of mind that Merton describes in any place. Searching for the right place is characteristic of the forever moving American society. There is no right place. We carry within ourselves both the right and the wrong places. We already have within that for which we search outside.

Americans who boast of being self-made are only making the best of what is given to them. With good fortune or luck, our mind and spirit lead the way. At best, we are inspired by

[1]Merton, Thomas. *Thoughts in Solitude*. Boston: Shambhala Pocket Classics, 1993, pp. 17, 18.

forces we do not know, but most of the time we only do the construction work based on the spiritual blueprints in our psyches. Nonetheless, it would be foolish to discount will and steadfast determination.

Montaigne has suggested that a man should keep for himself a little back shop, all his own, quite unadulterated, in which he establishes his true freedom and chief place of seclusion and solitude.[1]

Thomas Merton was not content with living with the silent monks at the monastery. He was able to have his own private hermitage on the grounds where he prayed, meditated, contemplated, and wrote. It is no accident that countless Americans eagerly read his autobiography, *The Seven Storey Mountain*, and his many books on the spiritual life. Here was a man who renounced the material and money-driven worlds, leaving the chaos of noise and competition to live out the innate human longing for silence submerged within us all. In addition, he could write in beautiful and powerful prose. It is important to mention that while he hoped that the monastery authorities would prohibit him from writing (that is, silence him), on the contrary they encouraged his writing. In his autobiography, there is the story of his psychoanalytic experience with Gregory Zilboorg, which was destructive and cruelly manipulative. At the end of his life, Merton (a devout Catholic) was drawn to Buddhism.

In Merton's biography by Michael Mott, the story of the destructive and cruel manipulations of the Freudian psychoanalyst Zilboorg is revealed.[2]

---

[1]Montaigne, Michel de. "Of Solitude" in *The Complete Works of Montaigne* translated by Donald M. Frame. Stanford, Calif.: Stanford University Press, 1957, p. 177.
[2]Mott, Michael. *The Seven Mountains of Thomas Merton*. Boston: Houghton Mifflin, 1984, pp. 290-99.

Entering the Contemplative Monastic Life

When Bernadette Roberts was six years old, she began to experience fleeting moments of silence. At the age of fifteen, she called these times her *blank mind*, moments of no-self, or floating on the sea. Roberts said they were like an immovable still point that was permanently silent and utterly peaceful. At seventeen, the still point vanished and she described a bottomless black hole at the center of her being. She found a priest of the silent Carmelite order, who told her that "the lower you go, the higher you rise." She entered the contemplative monastery where she had a revelation: "There was nothing *in* this silence, only silence itself. ... I would wonder where my silence left off and God's began. ..."

This silence was not a silence of the mind, "but a coming upon the permanent accessibility to the still point that can always be seen and into which the self can descend or dissolve through various levels and degrees of silence."

Roberts called her experience the "dark night of the soul," in which she was aware of being on the brink of insanity. This condition lasted nine months. When the journey ended, she realized that she had experienced "a silence of the self – the experience of No-Self."

Roberts described the journey's end:

I discovered the increasing ability to sustain more fully the general intensity, without the lights going out – that is, without going unconscious, blacking out, or dropping into a conscious darkness in which there is nothing at all. Thus, there came the necessary strength to bear the vision with full consciousness; in doing so, the awareness of everything else falls away – the body, surroundings, the silence, everything – and compared to this intensity, the loss of self is nothing, for man, indeed the whole universe, has more to lose than itself.[1]

[1]Roberts, Bernadette. *The Experience of No-Self: A Contemplative Journey.* Boston: Shambhala, 1984, pp. 19, 93-95.

It would be easy for me to explain this circumstance in terms of psychosis such as schizophrenia, since I have treated natural schizophrenia before there were drugs, but it is equally important to see it as a journey of the soul. Modern psychiatrists will never have the opportunity to see how the psyche processes such material because they only know drugged psychotic patients. This observation is not to disparage the antipsychotic medications, which have been a great boon to sufferers. From the point of view of this book, however, Roberts offers a unique experience of the human depth of silence and the healing power of the contemplative monastic life.

Bernadette Roberts' story grows to new heights in another book published one year later, after her experience with the Cistercian monks of St. Benedict's Monastery in Colorado. She formulates her ideas in greater depth and order in the battle between unknown forces. In her silence, she sees a new movement in the contemplative life and its journey with Christ after He gave up His self on the cross.[1]

Solitude

Philip Koch describes the philosophical encounter with solitude as "disengagement from people" and says that the silence, isolation, and reflection come from the core feature: the absence of others in one's experiential world. Koch concludes that "silence is the luminous silent space of freedom, of self and nature, reflection and creative power. There we feel and see with a freshness scarcely to be believed."[2]

The spiritual teacher, Ramana Maharishi, does not envision solitude as disengagement leading to the absence of others, but instead as detachment – regardless of whether

---

[1]Roberts, Bernadette. *The Path to No-Self: Life at the Center*. Boston: Shambhala, 1985.
[2]Koch, Philip. *Solitude: A Philosophical Encounter*. Peru, IL.: Open Court, 1994, p. 299.

other people are around or not. It is in the mind, and "one might be in the thick of the world and yet maintain perfect serenity of the mind; such a person is always in solitude."[1]

Anthony Storr, an English psychotherapist, attempts in his book on solitude to balance the one-sided psychoanalytic literature focusing on the fear of or wish for being alone by honoring the ability to be alone. Because of the noise of Western culture, people feel uncomfortable in its absence: "Hence the menace of 'Musak' has invaded shops, hotels, aircraft, and even elevators."

Storr said:

> Perhaps monastic discipline and the absence of close ties not only facilitated the individual's relationship with God, but also fostered scholarship. It would, I think, be quite wrong to assume that all those who have put their relations with God before their relations with their fellows as abnormal or neurotic.[2]

In 1995, I made a television interview in London with Baroness Vera von der Hydt, a ninety-two-year-old Jungian analyst. Our discussion was about her experience as an analysand of C. G. Jung, about her life, aging, and death. She wrote to me later:

> You asked me about silence when you were here. Silence is important to me. However, I chatter. I can chatter. At one point it was part of life, in a way a part of one's education. But I always seemed to know that it was something one 'put on' for a purpose, or for fun or duty – and it was split off from the core and therefore alienating. I am not sure if you can gather what I am trying to say. You see, I am grateful to be here in this convent. I do not have to talk to

---

[1]Maharishi, Ramana. "Silence and Solitude" in *The Spiritual Teaching of Ramana Maharishi*. Boston: Shambhala, 1988.
[2]Storr, Anthony. *Solitude: A Return to the Self*. New York: Free Press, 1988, p. 83.

the sisters, but, of course, sometimes it happens and although we may talk about the weather, there is an awareness of the silent core and talking is no longer a disturbance. ... May the stillness of silence always remain with you – finished book or not.

Love, Vera

The ideas of solitude and of being alone are inherently contradictory. For example, the physician, Sir Thomas Browne, in his famous book, *Religio Medici*, published in 1646, wrote:

There is no man alone, because every man is a microcosm, and carries the whole world about him ... though it be the apophthegm of a wise man, is yet true in the mouth of a fool; indeed though in a wilderness, a man is never alone, not only because he is with himself and his own thoughts, but because he is with the devil; whoever consorts with our solitude, and is that unruly rebel that musters up those disordered motions which accompany our sequestered imaginations. And to speak more narrowly, there is no such thing as solitude, nor any thing that can be said to be alone and by itself but God, who is his own circle and can subsist by himself. ... [1]

The late Octavio Paz, Nobel laureate for literature, wrote a book on Mexico's quest for identity, titled *The Labyrinth of Solitude*, in which he expressed his conviction:

Solitude – the feeling and knowledge that one is alone, alienated from the world and oneself – is not an exclusively Mexican characteristic. All men, at some moment in their lives, feel themselves to be alone. And they are. To live is to be separated from what we were in order to approach what we are going to be in the mysterious future. Solitude is the

---

[1]Browne, Sir Thomas. *Religio Medici*. New York: E. P. Dutton, n.d., pp. 129-30.

profoundest fact of the human condition. Man is the only being who knows he is alone, and the only one who seeks out another. His nature – if that word can be used in reference to man, who has "invented" himself by saying "No" to nature – consists in his longing to realize himself in another. Man is nostalgia and a search for communion. Therefore, when he is aware of himself he is aware of his lack of another, that is, his solitude.[1]

Thomas Merton says that in reality all men are solitary, but that most of them are so averse to being alone or feeling alone that they do anything they can to forget their solitude.[2]

Seeking Another and Sex

It would be the ultimate oversight to avoid speaking about man seeking woman, woman seeking man, and sex. While classical monastic life is celibate, today married men and women go to monasteries, alone or together, for solace and silence. The power of instinctual sexual energy and attraction is universal in human beings and animals. Its intensity varies at different ages and times in one's life. Human intercourse has biological, animal, physical drive, strong symbolic and mythical powers relating to the union of opposites, spirituality and an elemental relationship to birth and death.

Some of the drive to find the other is to counter being alone, rejected, unwanted, and incomplete. In Jungian psychology, this concept is theorizing in terms of the unconscious *anima*, or feminine archetype in men, and the *animus*, or unconscious masculine archetype in women. Regardless of the controversial aspects of this theory, it expresses an inner

---

[1]Paz, Octavio. *The Labyrinth of Solitude*. New York: Grove Weidenfeld, 1985, p. 195.
[2]Merton, Thomas. *Disputed Questions: The Philosophy of Solitude*. New York: Harcourt Brace Jovanovich, 1960, pp. 177-207.

reality in the form of the image of the idealized other sex for which we forever search to match with an outer real person.

Victor Hugo in *Les Misérables* wrote:

> The power of a glance has been so much abused in love stories, that it has come to be disbelieved in. Few people dare now to say that two human beings have fallen in love because they have looked at each other. Yet it is in this way that love begins, and in this way only. The rest is only the rest, and comes afterwards. Nothing is more real than these great shocks which two souls give each other in exchanging this spark.[1]

Freud broke the taboo about sex in the Victorian Age, shocking people with his theory of childhood sexuality. Sex was dominant in the minds of the psychoanalysts and usually their patients. I knew in my own Freudian analysis how everything seemed to get interpreted in the name of either resistance or the Oedipal complex. Cockwork was as sure as clockwork. I knew that I could talk about many things and my analyst would be mum, but talk about sex and I was certain to get a reaction.

We seek soul mates, but after the projections of the inner ideal woman or man are withdrawn when the real other person surfaces, problems emerge. It is only when those man/woman problems are worked out that a genuinely loving relationship can evolve. With our revolving door marriages, divorces, and more marriages, the vain search continues, as a rule, without being found in reality. Couples try to make each other over. Rationality succumbs to the power of our illogical unconscious. Both women and men become distorted images of themselves, wet by the extreme of feminism and of male chauvinism and power for possession and control.

I had a young woman patient who was constantly preoccupied by thoughts about sex during the day, and during her

---

[1]Hugo, Victor. *Les Misérables*. Translated by Charles E. Wilbour. New York: Modern Library, 1992, p. 775 (Part 4, Book III, vi).

restless sleep at night. She seemed enslaved by the idea that sexual relations with a man whom she would love was the only way to end her loneliness and longing. She was not promiscuous, and not a nymphomaniac, and seemed quite normal except for obsessive thoughts. They were like a noisy racket in her head. The idea of sex was on her mind and on her television all the time. She recounted the seven o'clock television show on a major network the night before I saw her. When she turned it on, she said, "There was a man energetically fucking a woman on top of his office desk." Seven o'clock! See, kids? See Dick run.

Sex is equated with noise, but love with silence and passionate intercourse, after the grunts, sighs, groans, and climax – a speechless oblivion. Sex is the central fact of our existence, the renewal of life, and the propagation of our species. Some wag defined the intellectual academic as someone who had found something more interesting than sex. Philip Barry described the togetherness of love as two minds without a single thought.[1]

When I was young and passionately in love with a beautiful woman, I was sitting alone with her trying with all my might to say, "I love you," but couldn't speak a word. The best I could do was – with great effort – make some sounds of disjointed sentences. This effort was total anguish. So we just sat without talking, looking deeply into each other's eyes. Much later she told me she had wanted to say, "You love me and can't get the words out. Come kiss me." Yet we parted with racing hearts but without talking. It was as if we had both hypnotized each other. When I was finally able to say to her, "I love you," I realized that, while she did love me, it was not like I loved her. No doubt that intuitive awareness had silenced me before.

Real lovers are comfortably silent. Lovemaking can be noisy and stimulated or cut off with words, but mostly it is silent. With the climax, it is as if the people and thinking have

[1]Barry, Philip, in *Dictionary of Quotations* edited by Bergen Evans. New York: Wings Books, 1969, p. 406: 21.

evaporated, and it is at these moments that we may experience extinction and death. The deepest love relationships are not expressed in talk, but in poetry, music, dance, and art – which are made powerful and meaningful by their MA pauses.

Togetherness of lovers requires its own MA. Listen to Kahlil Gibran's words from *The Prophet*:

> Ay, you shall be together even in the silent memory of God,
> But let there be spaces in your togetherness,
> And let the winds of the heavens dance between you. ...
> For the pillars of the temple stand apart,
> And the oak tree and the cypress grow not in each other's shadow.[1]

Kathleen Norris

Kathleen Norris published a best-selling autobiography, *Dakota*, in 1992 and a sequel, *The Cloister Walk*, in 1996. Born in the village of Lemmon, South Dakota, which now has a population of 1,700 people, she is a poet, married to a poet. Kathleen worked in New York City for six years before she moved back home. I invited her to speak at the Salado Institute on silence and her experience in a Benedictine monastery not far from her home. Norris, a Presbyterian who preaches at the Presbyterian church in Lemmon, also spends long periods in residence at the Benedictine monastery. For ten years, she had been a Benedictine oblate, having taken abbreviated but powerful monastic vows.

Although rooted in the Dakota prairie, she still likes to visit friends in New York City. She says, "I am conscious of carrying a plain's silence within me in cities, and carrying my city experiences back to the plains so that they may be absorbed again back into silence, fruitful silence that produces poems and essays."

In *The Cloister Walk*, she says:

[1]Gibran, Kahlil. *The Prophet*. New York: Knopf, 1958, p. 15.

"Listen" is the first word of St. Benedict's Rule for monasteries, and listening for the eruptions of grace into one's life – often from unlikely sources – is a "quality of attention" that both monastic living and the practice of writing tend to cultivate. I'm trained to listen when words and images begin to converge. When I wake up at 3 a.m., suddenly convinced that I had better look into an old notebook, or get to work on a poem I'd abandoned years before, I do not turn over and go back to sleep. I obey, which is an active form of listening.

In fact, I tell the monks, when I first encountered the ancient desert story about obedience – a monastic disciple is ordered by his abba to water a dead stick – I laughed out loud. I know abba's voice from these 3 a.m. encounters; I know the sinking, hopeless feeling that nothing could possibly come out of this writing I feel compelled to do. I also know that good things often come when I persevere. But it took a long time to recognize that my discipline as a writer, some of it at least, could translate into the monastic realm.[1]

Besides her personal contemplative silent retreats, Norris attends annual Benedictine community silent retreats with over one hundred women, many of whom work outside the convent as nurses, social workers, chaplains, and professors. She also lectures and spends time as a visiting artist in elementary schools.

Drawn to the Desert Fathers of the Benedictine Order, Norris speculates:

Maybe the desert wisdom of the Dakota can teach us to love anyway, to love what is dying, in the face of death, and not pretend that things are other than they are. The irony and wonder of all of this are that it is the desert's grimness, its stillness and isolation, that brings us back to love. Here

[1]Norris, Kathleen. *The Cloister Walk*. New York: Riverhead Books, 1996, pp. 143-44.

we discover the paradox of the contemplative life, that the desert of solitude can be the school where we learn to love others.

To live communally in silence is to admit new power into your life. In a sense you are giving silence its due. But the silence is not passive, and soon you realize that it has the power to change you.[1]

In patientia vestra habetis animam vestram[2]: An Alchemical Exhortation

Until now I have spoken of noise as a dark side of Americans' gap-filling society. As an introverted writer who cherishes silence to nurture the creative spirit, and as an analyst who treasures silence as the key to listening, I have invited your careful attention to the pauses, empty spaces, and Nothing which I identify as MA. I now call attention to the dark side of silence, which might be referred to as "Shadow Silence."

Using Jung's concept of the shadow archetype, I give you a common example of what I call Shadow Silence in the dark, abrupt silence that immediately follows the impatient, hostile blowing of an automobile horn meant to enrage another driver. It is safe to assume that the blasting sound is a nonverbal signal of the wish to kill another driver who is suddenly perceived as the enemy. Self-righteous horn blasters assume that they own the road, and take pride in being tough menaces. Such behavior epitomizes our cultural adversarial, in-your-face, confrontational bad manners.

Usually such high-speed highway events are triggered when one driver plugs the personal MA of another with his or her automobile. There is practically no more MA on our highways. The sound is a projection of the horn-blower's

---

[1]*Ibid.*
[2]"In your patience you will have your soul," from Aniela Jaffé, *Jung's Last Years*. Dallas, Texas: Spring Publications, 1984, p. 116.

shadow. When violent sound directed against an individual ends with sudden silence, the mind either goes dead or pulsates with anger, rage, and vengeance. This state is the legacy of Shadow Silence.

On the other hand, there is a genuine silence in the auto horn-blowing world: a nonshadow silence felt as miraculous relief after a driver has been alerted by a loud horn that prevented a disastrous collision. The opposite of Shadow Silence is the Spiritual Silence that I have described earlier.

We ordinarily understand shadow as the negative principle, as opposed to the positive principle of the sun. There can be no shadow without substance to cast it. In primitive societies, the shadow may represent witchcraft and spells. Thus, natives take great care where their shadows fall, and avoid walking into another person's shadow.

Jung defined that Shadow archetype as personifying the reprehensible tendencies of an individual, and the inferior traits of character which that person refuses to acknowledge about himself or herself. Nonetheless, they thrust themselves upon the person, directly or indirectly, as images and symbols of the Shadow. Various images of the Shadow appear menacingly in frightening nightmares, or are seen while we are awake as projections onto other people. How very convenient in our blame-obsessed society.

The Shadow, although it can appear as evil, is not synonymous with evil because in addition to our own worst selves, it can display our good qualities – such as normal instincts, appropriate reactions, realistic insights, and creative impulses. Even if it is bad, provided we are consciously aware, we are forced to acknowledge that the negative part of ourselves, which we wish to deny, still exists.[1]

---

[1]Jung, C. G. "The Archetype and the Collective Unconscious" in *Collected Works*, Vol. 9, i. Princeton, N.J.: Princeton University Press, 1970, p. 284, and *Aion*, Vol. 9, ii, Princeton, N.J.: Princeton University Press, 1971, Part 2, p. 266.

I cite a powerful description of the Shadow by the seventeenth-century doctor, Sir Thomas Browne:

> The heart of man is the place where the devils dwell in: The heart of man is deceitful above all things, and desperately wicked. I feel sometimes a hell within myself; Lucifer keeps his court in my breast; Legion is revived in me. There are as many hells as Anaxagoras' conceited worlds; there was more than one hell in Magdalene, when there were seven devils; for every devil is a hell unto himself; he holds enough of torture in his own ubi, and needs not the misery of circumference to afflict him and thus, a distracted conscience here is a shadow or introduction unto hell hereafter.[1]

Anaxagoras, a Greek philosopher who went to Athens in 300 B.C., published the revolutionary thesis that mind and matter exist as two distinct entities, and as a scientist, first explained the solar eclipses.

George Steiner, in his book, *Language and Silence: Essays on Language, Literature and the Inhuman*, presents a horrifying vision of the humanely educated Nazi. Steiner wrote that the most appalling brutalities of this century did not spring up in the Gobi Desert or the rainforests of the Amazon. They rose from within, and from the core of European civilization. The cries of the murdered sounded within earshot of the universities; the sadism went on a street away from the theaters and the museums.[2]

It is only fair to point out that Jung, father of the Shadow archetype, was sometimes blind to his own shadow, as with his projections on Albert Schweitzer. In a letter dated 23 September 1952, Jung writes that Schweitzer is urgently needed in Europe but prefers to be a touching savior of savages and to hang his theology on the wall. We have a justification for missionizing only when we have straightened

[1]Browne. *Religio Medici*, p. 89.
[2]Steiner, George. *Language and Silence: Essays on Language, Literature and the Inhuman*. New York: Atheneum, 1966.

ourselves out, Jung says, otherwise we are merely spreading our own disease.

On 9 September 1953, one year after Schweitzer was awarded the Nobel Prize for Peace, Jung wrote his private thoughts in a letter:

> Albert Schweitzer, by the way, would have deserved a reward for his courageous book on the Jesus biography research, but not on his African romance, which any little doctor could take care of as well without being made into a saint. It is mere escape from the problem called Europe.

In a letter written 11 December 1953, Jung said:

> I'm afraid I can only feel it as painful that Schweitzer found the answer to catastrophic conclusion in his Quest for the Historical Jesus in abandoning the cura animarum in Europe by becoming a white savior to the natives.[1]

Albert Schweitzer wrote about modern man in 1932, saying:

> Above all he is thus made capable of excusing everything that is meaningless, cruel, unjust, or bad in the behavior of his nation. Unconsciously to themselves, the majority of the members of our barbarian civilized states give less and less time to reflection as moral personalities, so that they may not be continually coming into inner conflict with their fellows as a body, and continually having to get over things which they feel to be wrong.[2]

I know of as many stupid and destructive actions by Jungian analysts as by Freudian psychoanalysts. Individual experiences are called anecdotes by scientifically minded

---

[1]Jung, C. G. *Letters*, Vol. 2: 1951-1961. Princeton, N.J.: Princeton University Press, 1975, pp. 85, 125, 140-42.
[2]Joy, Charles R. (Ed.) *Albert Schweitzer: An Anthology*. Boston: Beacon Press, 1959, p. 137.

observers, but it is our individual experience and personality that determine our life course. Statistics are sterile and probably meaningless when it comes down to the one person in front of you.

And What Can We Do About Silence and Noise?

I offer some practical advice, fully aware that no one takes suggestions who is not ready to accept them:

Find a silent space of your own and retreat to it from time to time. Seek solitude and Nature when urban life makes you weary. Forego the increasingly lush cruises and high-flying excitement. Welcome something low, neither costly nor glamorous. Search out your real self, and avoid sham. Facing up to hypocrisy is easy to say, but it is a critical breakthrough for growth and balance.

Find your own spirituality – and the simpler, less trendy or *de rigueur*, the better. Nurture skepticism of clichés, advertisements, and opinionated voices. Avoid a doomsday or darkly pessimistic attitude. Remember that there is nothing that cannot change – or no one. Do not be a fool trying to be a magician or miracle worker unless you have that genius and spirit within which characterize a truly great person. Avoid being inflated.

Take time, honor patience, and find your religious center. It probably is not in church. Listen! Listen! Listen! Quit talking so much. Read books instead of disappearing into television. Remember that the odd or unusual, the stranger, and people who are different from you may be essential to your humanity and salvation.

The Bible does not say that money is the source of all evil, but it says that *the love of money* is the source of all evil.

It is a safe bet that what or whom you hate most is your *bête noire* or black beast, a projection of your own shadow. Shadow is the source of most of the noise in human relations. Call it prejudice if you wish, but remember to look within yourself for what you hate or despise without. We do not hate that which is not important to us. We are just indifferent to it. We hate it, them, him, or her because they disappoint us in not delivering to us what we feel they ought to give us.

Americans want silence insofar as it involves silencing other people and not themselves. In our American argumentative culture, we have fallen in love with adversarial states of mind that cherish opposition as the way to get things done. We debate and do not talk. The media extol polarized views, verbal attack and mean accusations.[1]

While sometimes it is wise to talk, to argue, to make your point with all the vigor and noise you can muster, pick those times carefully. There are few times in life when you can prove that you are right.

Given a chance, create a place of silence – an island or oasis for silent listening – and invite friends to gather.

The Quest for Silence

> A prudent silence is the sacred vessel of wisdom.[2]

The word *quest* suggests a mystical pursuit, following an inspiration or vocation – a calling. A *quester* implies a disciplined searcher for a truth. The dictionary defines *quest* as an inquiry, investigation, or search, and in medieval times, as the adventures of knights. A memorable illustration is Sir Lancelot's quest for the Holy Grail – which is less about obtaining the Grail itself than the redemption that accompanies it. In the Legend of King Arthur, finding the Holy Grail and the Bleeding Spear led to the miraculous healing of the King's seemingly incurable wound.

---

[1]See Deborah Tannen's book, *The Argument Culture: Moving from Debate to Dialogue.* New York: Random House, 1998.
[2]Fischer, Martin. *The Gracian Manual: Baltasar Gracian, A Truthtelling Manual and the Art of Worldly Wisdom* [1653]. Springfield, IL.: Charles C. Thomas, 1945, No. 3.

Then Galahad set the Grail upon the altar and knelt once more in prayer. And as he knelt, his life was accomplished, and his soul was taken up to Heaven so that his body lay dead before the altar. Then the sunbeam descended from above, striking clean through the roof of the chapel, and the Bleeding Spear and the Holy Grail passed up and vanished from sight, nor were they ever seen again upon this earth.[1]

I have tried to convey the quintessential importance of silent spaces, and necessary pauses.

So, now, I suggest:

> Turn off the radio.
> Turn off the television.
>
> Sit quietly in your chosen place of solitude.
> Let your inner self speak to you.
> Listen patiently into silence.
>
> When calmness comes,
> Then you will have used your will to
> Let silence befriend you
> Before and while you speak.

[1]Green, Roger Lancelyn. *King Arthur and His Knights of the Round Table.* Baltimore: Penguin Books, 1955, p. 247.

Bibliography

Ambrose, Stephen. *Undaunted Courage: Meriwether Lewis, Thomas Jefferson, and the Opening of the American West*. New York: Touchstone Books, 1996.

Azizuki, Tatsuichiro. *Nagasaki 1945*. London: Quartet Books, 1981.

Barry, Philip, in *Dictionary of Quotations* edited by Bergen Evans. New York: Wings Books, 1969.

Barbree, Jay, and Martin Caidin. *A Journey Through Time: Exploring the Universe with the Hubble Space Telescope*. New York: Penguin Studio, 1995.

Barzun, Jacques. Seminar at the Institute for the Humanities at Salado (Salado, Texas), November 20, 1988.

Becker, Ernest. *The Denial of Death*. New York: Free Press, 1973.

Beckett, Samuel. *Molly* in *Three Novels by Samuel Beckett*. New York: Grove Press, 1965.

Brodsky, Joseph. *A Part of Speech*. New York: Strauss and Giroux, 1986.

Brown, Michael. Address at the Institute for the Humanities at Salado (Salado, Texas), November 3, 1996.

Browne, Sir Thomas. *Religio Medici*. New York: E. P. Dutton, n. d.

Buber, Martin. *I and Thou*, 2nd ed. New York: Charles Scribner's Sons, 1958.

Burke, Edmund. *On the Sublime and Beautiful: Harvard Classics*, Vol. 24. New York: P. F. Collier and Son, 1909.

Cage, John. *Silence for a Speaker*. Middletown, Conn.: Wesleyan University Press, 1961.

Carlyle, Thomas. *Sartor Resartus*. New York: Dutton, 1973.

Carpenter, Edmund. *They Became What They Beheld*. New York: Ballantine Books, 1970.

Carroll, Lewis. *Through the Looking Glass: And What Alice Found There*. New York: Julian Messner, 1982.

Chism, Olin. "Takemitsu and Gould: A Final Note" in *Dallas Morning News*, March 3, 1996.

Chopra, Deepak. *Quantum Healing: Exploring the Frontiers of Mind/ Body Medicine.* New York: Bantam, 1989.

Cleland, Max. *Strong at the Broken Places: A Personal Story.* New York: Berkley Books, 1982.

— Seminar at the Institute for the Humanities at Salado (Salado, Texas), November 19, 1995 (transcript of tape recording).

Cohen, J. M., and Phipps. *The Common Experience.* Los Angeles: Tarcher, 1979.

Davies, Robertson. *The Merry Heart: Reflections on Reading, Writing, and the World of Books.* New York: Viking/Penguin, 1996.

DeMuth, Philip. "Eliza and Her Offspring" in *Literature and Medicine,* Vol. 4: *Psychiatry and Medicine* edited by Peter W. Graham. Baltimore: Johns Hopkins University Press, 1985.

Eckhart, Meister. (Translated by R. B. Blakney.) New York: Harper & Row, 1941.

Einstein, Albert, in *Man and the Universe: The Philosophy of Science* edited by Saxe Commins and Robert N. Linscott. New York: Random House, 1947.

Eliade, Mercea. *Yoga: Immortality and Freedom, 2nd ed.* Princeton, N.J.: Princeton University Press, 1973.

Eliot, T. S. *Four Quartets.* New York: Harcourt Brace Jovanovich, 1971.

— *T. S. Eliot: Selected Poems.* New York: Harcourt, Brace and World, 1964.

Evans, Bergen. *Dictionary of Mythology.* New York: Dell, 1972.

Feikema, Feike. *Boy Almighty.* St. Paul, Minn.: Itasca Press, 1945.

Feld, Steven. *Sound and Sentiment: Birds, Weeping, Poetics, and Song in Kaluli Expression.* Philadelphia: University of Pennsylvania Press, 1982.

Fisher, Martin. *The Gracian Manual: Baltasar Gracian, A Truthtelling Manual and the Art of Worldly Wisdom* [1653], No. 3. Springfield, IL.: Charles C. Thomas, 1945.

Freud. Sigmund. *The Complete Psychological Works of Sigmund Freud, Standard Edition,* Vol. XI. London: Hogarth Press, 1957.

Frye, Northup. *Anatomy of Criticism: Four Essays.* Princeton, N.J.: Princeton University Press, 1973.

Ghiselin, Brewster (Ed.) *The Creative Process: A Symposium.* New American Library, 1952.

Gibran, Kahlil. *The Prophet.* New York: Knopf, 1958.

— *The Vision: Reflections on the Way of the Soul.* Ashland, Oregon: White Cloud Press, 1994.

Goethe, Wolfgang Johann. *Faust:* Harvard Classics, Vol. 19. New York: P. F. Collier and Son, 1909.

Green, Roger Lancelyn. *King Arthur and His Knights of the Round Table.* Baltimore: Penguin Books, 1955.

Henderson, Harold G. *An Introduction to Haiku.* Garden City, N.Y.: Doubleday Anchor Books, 1958.

Hendricks, Robert G. *Te-Tao Ching: "A New Translation of the Ma-Wang-Tue Text."* New York: Ballantine Books, 1989.

Herberg, Will. *The Writings of Martin Buber.* New York: Meridian Books, 1956. Hersey, John H. *Hiroshima.* New York: Bantam, 1979.

Hoffer, Eric. *Before the Sabbath.* New York: Harper & Row, 1979.

Hood, Thomas. "Silence," sonnet in *John Bartlett's Familiar Quotations.* Boston: Little, Brown, 1940.

Hugo, Victor. *Les Misérables.* Translated by Charles E. Wilbour. New York: Modern Library, 1992.

Jaffé, Aniela. *From the Life and Work of C.G. Jung.* Einsiedeln: Daimon, 1989.

Jenning, Humphrey. *Pandemonium 1660-1896: The Coming of the Machine as Seen by Contemporary Observers.* New York: Free Press, 1985.

Joy, Charles R. (Ed.). *Albert Schweitzer: An Anthology.* Boston: Beacon Press, 1959.

Jung, C. G. *Letters*, Vol. 2: 1951-1961. (Edited by Gerhard Adler). Princeton, N.J.: Princeton University Press, 1975.

— *Collected Works.* Princeton, N.J.: Princeton University Press, 1979.

— Foreword to *Zen Buddhism* by D. T. Suzuki. New York: Grove Press, 1964.

— *Word and Image,* edited by Aniela Jaffé. Princeton, N.J.: Princeton University Press, 1979.

— *Studies in Word Association.* London: Routledge & Kegan Paul, 1969 [first published in 1918].

— "Dream Analysis" (seminars, mimeograph of original), Vol. 3, 1929.

— "The Archetype and the Collective Unconscious" in *Collected Works of C. G. Jung*, Vol. 9, i. Princeton, N.J.: Princeton University Press, 1971.

Kaufmann, Walter (Ed.) "The Gay Science" in *The Portable Nietzsche* by Friedrich Wilhelm Nietzsche. New York: Viking, 1954.

Koch, Philip. *Solitude: A Philosophical Encounter*. Peru, IL.: Open Court, 1994.

Kuramitsu, Osamu. Personal conversation with Harry Wilmer, Salado, Texas, 1997.

Lacout, Pierre. *God Is Silence*. London: Friends Home Service Committee, 1969.

Lanier, Emilio, cited by Edmund Carpenter on "Interval" in *They Became What They Beheld*. New York: Ballantine, 1970.

Laurents, Arthur. *Home of the Brave: A Play in Three Acts (Acting Edition)*. Dramatists Play Service, 1945.

Lerner, Alan Jay. *My Fair Lady* (adaptation and lyrics). New York: Coward-McCann, 1956. (Music by Frederick Lowe).

Lévi-Strauss, Claude. *The Raw and the Cooked: Introduction to a Science of Mythology*. New York: Harper & Row, 1969.

Lincoln, Abraham. "The Gettysburg Address" in *Famous Speeches of Abraham Lincoln*. Mount Vernon, N.Y.: Peter Pauper Press, 1935.

Magill, Frank N. *Masterpieces of World Literature*. New York: Harper & Row, 1989.

Maharishi, Ramana. *Silence and Solitude: The Spiritual Teaching of Ramana Maharishi*. Boston: Shambhala, 1988.

McGuire, William, and R. F. C. Hull (Eds.). *Jung Speaking: Interviews and Encounters*. Princeton, N.J.: Princeton University Press, 1977.

Mellick, Jill. *The Natural Artistry of Dreams: Creative Ways to Bring the Wisdom of Dreams to Waking Life*. Berkeley, Calif.: Corari Press, 1996.

Melville, Herman. *Billy Budd*. New York: New American Library, 1961.

Merker, Hannah. *Listening: Ways of Hearing in a Silent World*. New York: Harper-Collins, 1994.

Merton, Thomas. *The Seven Storey Mountain*. New York: Signet Books/New American Library, 1962.

— *The Way of Chuang Tzu*. Boston: Shambhala, 1991.

— *Thoughts in Solitude*. Boston: Shambhala Pocket Classics, 1993.

— *Disputed Questions: The Philosophy of Silence*. New York: Harcourt Brace Jovanovich, 1960.

Milne, A. A. *The House at Pooh Corner*. New York: Dutton, 1928.

Milton, John. *Paradise Lost:* Harvard Classics, Vol. 4. New York: P. F. Collier and Son, 1909.

Montaigne, Michel de. "Of Solitude" in *The Complete Works of Montaigne* translated by Donald M. Frame. Stanford, Calif.: Stanford University Press, 1957.

Mott, Michael. *The Seven Mountains of Thomas Merton*. Boston: Houghton Mifflin, 1984.

Nietzsche, Friedrich Wilhelm. "Thus Spake Zarathustra" in *The Portable Nietzsche* (Walter Kaufmann, ed.). New York: Viking, 1954.

Nightingale, Benedict. *New York Times*, "Theater," February 26, 1984. *The New Shorter Oxford English Dictionary*, Vols. I and II. Oxford, England: Clarendon Press, 1993.

Norris, Kathleen. *The Cloister Walk*. New York: Riverhead Books, 1996.

Olsen, Tillie. *Silences*. New York: Dell, 1978.

Ortega y Gasset, José. *Man and People*. New York: W. W. Norton, 1957. *Oxford English Dictionary, Compact Edition*, Vols. I and II. Oxford, England: Oxford University Press, 1979.

Paz, Octavio. *The Labyrinth of Solitude*. New York: Grove Weidenfeld, 1985.

Penrose, Roger. *The Emperor's New Mind: Concerning Computers, Minds, and Laws of Physics*. New York: Oxford University Press, 1989.

Picard, Max. *The World of Silence*. Washington, D. C.: Regnery Gateway, 1988.

Pilgrim, Richard. "Intervals (Ma) in Space and Time: Foundations for a Religio-Aesthetic Paradigm in Japan" in *History of Religion*, Vol. 18 (1986).

Redner, Harry. *In the Beginning Was the Deed: Reflections on the Passage of Faust*. Berkeley, Calif.: University of California Press, 1982.

Reik, Theodor. *Listening with the Third Ear: The Inner Experience of a Psychoanalyst*. 1948 (Noonday Press, 1963).

Remarque, Eric Maria. *All Quiet on the Western Front*. Boston: Little Brown, 1929.

Richardson, Boyce. *People of Terra Nullus: Betrayal and Rebirth in Aboriginal Canada*. Seattle: University of Washington Press, 1993.

Roberts, Bernadette. *The Experience of No-Self: A Contemplative Journey.* Boston: Shambhala, 1984.

— *The Path to No-Self: Life at the Center.* Boston: Shambhala, 1985.

Russell, Jeffrey Burton. *A History of Heaven: The Singing Silence.* Princeton, N.J.: Princeton University Press, 1997.

Schnetzler, Jean-Pierre. *"Le Silence de la Psychanalyse à la Méditation,"* Cahiers de Psychologie Jungienne, No. 44, 1985.

Seale, Avrel. "Sipping Tea with Elspeth Rostow" in *Alcalde*, January 1996, Vol. 84, No. 3.

Shakespeare, William. *Hamlet.* New York: Bantam, 1988.

Singer, Isaac Bashevis, with Richard Burgin. *Conversations with Isaac Bashevis Singer.* New York: Straus and Giroux, 1985.

Steiner, George. *No Passion Spent.* New Haven, Conn.: Yale University Press, 1996.

— *Language and Silence: Essays on Language, Literature and the Inhuman.* New York: Atheneum, 1966.

Stevenson, William. *A Man Named Intrepid: The Secret War.* New York: Ballantine, 1982.

Storr, Anthony. *Solitude: A Return to the Self.* New York: Free Press, 1988.

Stuckey, Charles F. *Monet: Water Lilies.* New York: Park Lane, 1988.

Suzuki, D. T. *Zen Buddhism.* Garden City, N.Y.: Doubleday Anchor Books, 1956.

Tannen, Deborah. *The Argument Culture: Moving from Debate to Dialogue.* New York: Random House, 1998.

Trumbo, Dalton. *Johnny Got His Gun.* New York: Citadel Press, 1991.

Twain, Mark. "Introductions" in *Speeches*, 1923.

— *On Writing and Publishing.* New York: Book of the Month Club, 1994.

van der Post, Sir Laurens. "The Dreamer that Remains" in *The Rock Rabbit and the Rainbow.* Einsiedeln, Switzerland: Daimon Verlag, 1998.

Ward, J. A. *American Silences: The Realm of James R. Walker, Evans and Edward Hopper.* Baton Rouge, La.: Louisiana State University Press, 1985.

Washkow, Arthur. Interview with Martin Marty in *Context*, April 1996.

Wayne, John. Source unknown.

Weinberg, Steven. *The First Three Minutes: A Modern View of the Origin of the Universe.* New York: Bantam, 1980.

Welch, Holmes. *Taoism: The Parting of the Way.* Boston: Beacon Press, 1966.

Wiesel, Elie. *Night.* New York: Bantam Books, 1986.

— "School of Works" in *Somewhere a Master: Further Hasidic Portraits and Legends.* New York: Summit Books, 1982.

Wilmer, Harry. *Social Psychiatry in Action: A Therapeutic Community.* Springfield, IL.: Charles C. Thomas, 1958.

— *Huber the Tuber: The Lives and Loves of a Tubercle Bacillus.* New York: National Tuberculosis Association, 1942.

— *Practical Jung: Nuts and Bolts of Jungian Psychotherapy.* Wilmette, IL.: Chiron Publications, 1987.

— *The Healing Nightmare.* A book in process.

— "The Healing Nightmare," Chapter 6 in *Trauma and Dreams* edited by Deirdre Barrett. Cambridge, Mass.: Harvard University Press, 1996.

— "The Healing Nightmare: A Study of the War Dreams of Vietnam Combat Veterans" in *Quadrant*, Vol. 19, Spring 1986.

— "A Hitherto Undescribed Island: An Approach to the Problem of Acculturation," *American Scientist*, Vol. 41, No. 3, July 1953.

— *How Dreams Help.* Einsiedeln: Daimon, 1999.

— *Understandable Jung: The Personal Side of Jungian Psychology*, Wilmette, Il.: Chiron Publications, 1994.

Wood, Ernest. *Yoga.* New York: Penguin Books, 1968.

Zenkei Shibayama (Nanzenji Monastery, Kyoto, Japan). Zen Mondo in *A Flower Does Not Talk.* Rutland, Vermont: Charles E. Tuttle, 1972.

Zenrin in *The Way of Zen* by Alan W. Watts. New York: New American Library/Mentor Book, 1957.

Zohar, Danah, in collaboration with I. N. Marshall. *The Quantum Self: Human Nature and Consciousness Defined by the New Physics.* New York: Morrow, 1990.

Index

About the Author

Harry Wilmer is founder, emeritus director, and president of the Institute for the Humanities at Salado, a small central Texas village where he has lived since 1971. Wilmer is a senior Jungian analyst in private practice in Salado, and spends mornings and evenings writing books, articles, and poetry, as well as illustrating his books.

He received his B.S., M.S., M.B., M.D., and Ph.D. degrees from the University of Minnesota. While interning in the Panama Canal Zone, he contracted tuberculosis. He spent one year at Glen Lake and Trudeau sanataria. After recovery, Wilmer became an instructor in pathology at the University of Minnesota, a National Research Council fellow in the medical sciences at Johns Hopkins Hospital, fellow in internal medicine and neuropsychiatry at the Mayo Clinic, and later a consultant in psychiatry at Mayo.

During the Korean War, he was in the Navy and retired as captain. His creative work in the Navy was the subject of an award-winning ABC docudrama, starring Lee Marvin with Arthur Kennedy as Wilmer. Bill Moyers produced two PBS-TV documentaries on Wilmer's work at the Salado Institute.

Wilmer is married to Jane Harris. They raised five children.

RECENT TITLES FROM **DAIMON**

Harry Wilmer

How Dreams Help

Harry Wilmer

HOW DREAMS HELP

Growing numbers of people are fascinated by the dream world. From psychological scholars and analysts to spontaneous groups and cults, the dream has a compelling voice. ... I make the point in this book that our dreams are our most creative inner source of wisdom and hope. ... The criterion for selection is simply that each one illustrates a common human life experience that all readers have had or are likely to have.

(from the Introduction)

From the Contents:
– Learning from Our Animal Natures: The Cat and the Jackass
– The Pleaser: Women Who Must Perform for Men
– She Who Must Be Right Will Admit No Error
– A Nightmare That Changed World History:
– Everyone Has a Pearl Harbor: The Talking Cat
– The Devil Made Me Do It: Encounter with the Trickster
– Family Values: When Being Bad May Be Good
– Relinquishing Power: Stepping Down

Eva Langley-Dános

Prison on Wheels – From Ravensbrück to Burgau

Prison on Wheels is a remarkable diary kept by a young Hungarian woman, Eva Dános, during sixteen horror-filled days and nights of deportation by the Nazis in 1945. It is an eyewitness report of a 700-kilometer rail journey from Ravensbrück, north of Berlin, to Burgau, near Munich, one of the countless such operations that took place within Nazi Germany's vast network of labor- and concentration-camps.

(128 pages, ISBN 3-85630-585-8)

RECENT TITLES FROM **DAIMON**

Ann and Barry Ulanov

The Healing Imagination – The Meeting of Psyche and Soul

This eloquent work speaks of the centrality of imagination in the life of the spirit. Ann and Barry Ulanov describe the imagination as a bridge between the psyche and the spirit.

Using rich imagery drawn from literature, film, and their own experience as therapists, they unlock for us the healing power of our imagination.

"Imagination heals by building a bridge sturdy enough to link us up, each of us, to the river of being already present in us, to the currents flowing through us and among us in our unconscious life."

After describing this healing power of imagination, the authors go on to show how it is vital in the spiritual life: in preaching, prayer, teaching, counseling, and politics.   (200 pages, ISBN 3-85630-591-2)

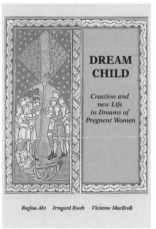

Regina Abt, Irmgard Bosch & Vivienne MacKrell

Dream Child – Creation and New Life in Dreams of Pregnant Women

Foreword by Marie-Louise von Franz
The broad scope of the dream material analyzed in this book allows the authors to touch upon many subjects associated with the nature of the psyche, not only those relevant to pregnant women. The careful interpretation of the amplificatory material drawn from a wide range of cultures also makes this an inspiring aid for the understanding of dreams, valuable to psychologists, doctors, midwives or anyone else interested in this human subject.

(ca. 500 pages, richly illustrated, ISBN 3-85630-592-0)

Images, Meanings and Connections

Essays in Memory of Susan R. Bach
Edited by Ralph Goldstein

The title of this book reflects the main themes from 50 years of Susan Bach's analytical work with spontaneous pictures and in her 'blue room.' In working with spontaneous pictures and drawings, she perceived the expression of deep connections between psyche and soma and learned that 'it knows within us' when either healing or death is imminent.

Talking with Susan Bach about her work was inspiring and humbling and one felt deeply privileged to be studying with someone who brought so much intuition and intellectual understanding to the contemplation of the human psyche.

The humbling part of the conversation came from wondering how to move one's own work towards the paths she was opening up. The purpose of this collection of essays is to show how the work of connecting and finding meaning continues and advances, whether through pictures, objects, dreams or other images and myths.

The contributors have in common both a Jungian orientation and their having made distinguished contributions in their own specialities. (ISBN 3-85630-586-6, 192 pages, richly illustrated)

Available from your bookstore or from our distributors:

In the United States:

Continuum
P.O. Box 7017
La Vergne, TN 37086
Phone: 800-937 5557
Fax: 615-793 3915

Chiron Publications
400 Linden Avenue
Wilmette, IL 60091
Phone: 800-397 8109
Fax: 847-256 2202

In Great Britain:

Airlift Book Company
8 The Arena
Enfield, Middlesex EN3 7NJ
Phone: (0181) 804 0400
Fax: (0181) 804 0044

Worldwide:

Daimon Verlag   Hauptstrasse 85   CH-8840 Einsiedeln   Switzerland
Phone: (41)(55) 412 2266   Fax: (41)(55) 412 2231
e-mail: info@daimon.ch   Write for our complete catalog!
www.daimon.ch

ENGLISH PUBLICATIONS BY **DAIMON**

Abt / Bosch / MacKrell *Dream Child – Creation and New Life in Dreams of Pregnant Women*
Susan R. Bach
- *Life Paints its Own Span*
- *Images, Meanings and Connections (ed. by Ralph Goldstein)*
E.A. Bennet
- *Meetings with Jung*
George Czuczka
- *Imprints of the Future*
Heinrich Karl Fierz
- *Jungian Psychiatry*
von Franz / Frey-Rohn / Jaffé
- *What is Death?*
Liliane Frey-Rohn
- *Friedrich Nietzsche*
Yael Haft
- *Hands: Archetypal Chirology*
Siegmund Hurwitz
- *Lilith, the First Eve*
Aniela Jaffé *From the Life und Work of C.G. Jung*
- *The Myth of Meaning*
- *Was C.G. Jung a Mystic?*
- *Death Dreams and Ghosts*
Verena Kast
- *A Time to Mourn*
- *Sisyphus*
Hayao Kawai *Dreams, Myths and Fairy Tales in Japan*
James Kirsch
- *The Reluctant Prophet*
Yehezkel Kluger & Nomi Kluger-Nash *A Psychological Interpretation of Ruth*
Mary Lynn Kittelson
- *Sounding the Soul*
Rivkah Schärf Kluger
- *The Gilgamesh Epic*
Paul Kugler *Jungian Perspectives on Clinical Supervision*
Eva Langley-Dános
- *Prison on Wheels: From Ravensbrück to Burgau*

Rafael López-Pedraza
- *Hermes and His Children*
- *Cultural Anxiety*
Gitta Mallasz (Transcription)
- *Talking with Angels*
Alan McGlashan *The Savage and Beautiful Country*
- *Gravity and Levity*
C.A. Meier
- *Healing Dream and Ritual*
- *A Testament to the Wilderness*
- *Personality*
Laurens van der Post
- *The Rock Rabbit and the Rainbow*
Rainer-Maria Rilke
- *Duino Elegies*
Miguel Serrano
- *C.G. Jung and Hermann Hesse: A Record of Two Friendships*
Helen Shulman
- *Living at the Edge of Chaos*
Susan Tiberghien
- *Looking for Gold*
Ann Ulanov
- *The Wizards' Gate*
- *The Female Ancestors of Christ*
Ann & Barry Ulanov
- *Cinderella and Her Sisters*
- *The Healing Imagination*
Erlo van Waveren
- *Pilgrimage to the Rebirth*

Jungian Congress Papers:

Jerusalem 1983 *Symbolic and Clinical Approaches*
Berlin 1986 *Archetype of Shadow in a Split World*
Paris 1989
- *Dynamics in Relationship*
Chicago 1992
- *The Transcendent Function*
Zürich 1995 *Open Questions in Analytical Psychology*
Florence 1998
- *Destruction and Creation*